PROJECT AIR FORCE

# Hybrid Warfare in the Baltics

## Threats and Potential Responses

Andrew Radin

Prepared for the United States Air Force

For more information on this publication, visit www.rand.org/t/RR1577

Library of Congress Cataloging-in-Publication Data is available for this publication.
ISBN: 978-0-8330-9558-9

Published by the RAND Corporation, Santa Monica, Calif.
© Copyright 2017 RAND Corporation
RAND® is a registered trademark.

Cover: *REUTERS/Ints Kalnins.*

**Support RAND**
Make a tax-deductible charitable contribution at
www.rand.org/giving/contribute

www.rand.org

# Preface

This report documents research performed by RAND Project AIR FORCE in the spring and summer of 2015. The report examines the specific challenges associated with Russian hybrid warfare in the Baltics—defining the issue, understanding the threat, and conceptualizing how to respond. It finds that Russia will have difficulty using nonviolent or covert action to subvert the Baltics absent the use of conventional force, and hence that the main vulnerability stems from Russia's local superiority in conventional forces. Addressing the Russian irregular threat remains important nevertheless, since effective defense and deterrence in the Baltics depend on adopting policies to reduce the likelihood of Russian aggression across the conflict spectrum.

The research described in this report was conducted within the Strategy and Doctrine Program of RAND Project AIR FORCE as part of a Fiscal Year 2015 project "U.S. Airpower and Moscow's Emerging Strategy in the Near Abroad." The project was sponsored by the Director, Plans, Programs, and Analyses, Headquarters United States Air Forces, Europe. Its goal was to help inform choices by U.S. Air Force leaders regarding ways—activities, posture, and capability development—in which the U.S. Air Force, U.S. Department of Defense, and the NATO alliance more broadly might respond to and anticipate challenges posed by a more assertive and bellicose Russian Federation.

Human Subject Protections (HSP) protocols were used in this report, in accordance with the appropriate statutes and Department of Defense regulations governing HSP. The views of individuals cited anonymously (as well as the views of the author) are their own, and do not represent the official position of the Department of Defense, the U.S. Government, or other organization.

## RAND Project AIR FORCE

RAND Project AIR FORCE (PAF), a division of the RAND Corporation, is the U.S. Air Force's federally funded research and development center for studies and analyses. PAF provides the Air Force with independent analyses of policy alternatives affecting the development, employment, combat readiness, and support of current and future air, space, and cyber forces. Research is conducted in four programs: Force Modernization and Employment; Manpower, Personnel, and Training; Resource Management; and Strategy and Doctrine. The research reported here was prepared under contract number FA7014-06-C-0001.

Additional information about PAF is available on our website: www.rand.org/paf

This report documents work originally shared with the U.S. Air Force on September 20, 2015. The draft report, issued on October 19, 2015, was reviewed by formal peer reviewers and U.S. Air Force subject-matter experts.

# Contents

# Summary

Many policymakers and analysts have expressed concerns about Russian use of "hybrid warfare," best understood as covert or deniable activities, supported by conventional or nuclear forces, to influence the domestic politics of target countries. These tactics are of particular concern in the Baltic countries of Estonia and Latvia, which have significant Russian-speaking minorities. To analyze the potential threat, I divide potential Russian hybrid aggression into three categories: nonviolent subversion, covert violent actions, and conventional warfare supported by subversion. Given the gains in standard of living and increasing integration of many Russian speakers in the Baltics, Russia will likely have difficulty using nonviolent tactics to destabilize these countries. Russian covert violent action is also unlikely to succeed on its own, given preparations by the security forces of Estonia and Latvia to "shoot" Russian "little green men"—meaning Russian forces that are covertly or unofficially deployed. The preparedness and relative competence of these security forces would likely compel Russia to choose between losing the conflict or escalating to conventional war with NATO members. The main vulnerability of the Baltics therefore lies in Russia's local conventional superiority. A large-scale conventional Russian incursion into the Baltics, legitimized and supported by political subversion, would rapidly overwhelm NATO forces currently postured in the region. If NATO leaders are to have confidence in their ability to deter such an attack, they will likely need to deploy additional forces to the region and to improve certain capabilities within their forces.

The United States and its NATO allies nevertheless should address the potential for all forms of Russian aggression across the conflict spectrum, in order to reduce the likelihood of miscalculation and to strengthen deterrence and defense in the region. To this end, this report offers three main recommendations for consideration by policymakers:

- First, the United States and NATO should pursue the development of a more sophisticated and subtle strategic communication campaign, beginning with support for Russian-language television stations backed by the Baltic country governments.
- Second, NATO should do more to strengthen the Baltic countries' security forces and thereby reduce the potential for Russian covert action.
- Third, the United States and NATO should take action to mitigate the risks that a NATO deployment in the Baltics will increase the potential for low-level Russian aggression. To this end, the United States and NATO should avoid basing forces in Russian-dominated areas, should consider measures to increase transparency or avoid the perception that deployed forces may be used to pursue regime change, and should develop a sound public relations campaign to convince local Russian speakers that NATO is not deploying forces against them.

# Acknowledgments

I would like to thank the sponsors for initiating and supporting this project. I would also like to thank David Ochmanek, the project leader, for his consistent and invaluable insight, advice, and encouragement. Further, my thanks go to Bryan Frederick for his comments, to Thomas Szayna for helping develop many of ideas contained here during our visit to the Baltics, and to James Torr and Natalie Ziegler for editing support. I also very much appreciate two detailed and very helpful reviews from Christopher Chivvis and Paul Stronski. Any errors are of course my own responsibility.

# 1. Introduction

Following Russia's covert actions and eventual annexation of Crimea, and its support for a separatist insurgency in eastern Ukraine, many policymakers and analysts have expressed concerns about Russian use of "hybrid warfare."[1] The Baltic countries of Estonia and Latvia are thought to be particularly vulnerable to this threat, which is best understood as the use of covert or deniable activities, supported by conventional or nuclear forces, to influence the domestic politics of target countries. Estonia and Latvia are NATO members, bordering Russia, with sizable Russian minorities. There is concern that Russia will seek to use the Russian minority to gain influence in the Baltics, use covert action to seize territory, use subversion to justify a conventional attack, or otherwise use deniable or convert means to gain influence in the Baltics and undermine the EU and NATO. At the heart of many analysts' and policymakers' concern is a fear that Russian actions will appear ambiguous, which may impede a response from the EU and NATO, given the need for consensus for a decision by these organizations.[2] Russia could hypothetically gain influence in the government in the Baltic countries, support a separatist region, or capture territory, thereby demonstrating the failure of the alliance's commitment to its eastern-most allies, undermining the larger agenda of Euro-Atlantic enlargement, and damaging U.S. credibility more widely.

At the same time, there are significant questions regarding how serious the threat of hybrid warfare in and of itself may be, especially compared with the threats posed by Russian conventional forces. Estonian and Latvian defense leaders claim that they are not especially worried about the hybrid threat and are more concerned about the prospect of a large-scale conventional attack.[3] Others argue that the term *hybrid warfare* is vague and unhelpful, and in any case the concepts that the term seeks to address are not especially novel.[4] These critiques raise questions such as what exactly the "hybrid" threat is, how the United States and NATO should respond, and how responding to the hybrid threat may relate to efforts to deter attacks or coercion by conventional forces. This report addresses these questions in the case of the Baltics, drawing on the record of Russian aggression in Ukraine, the discussion of hybrid warfare and related terms in the literature, the demographic and political context of the Baltics, and interviews with Baltic and NATO policymakers.

---

[1] Nadia Schadlow, "The Problem with Hybrid Warfare," *War on the Rocks*, April 2, 2015; Robert Coalson, "Top Russian General Lays Bare Putin's Plan for Ukraine," *The World Post*, September 2, 2014.

[2] James Sherr, for example, writes that hybrid warfare is "designed to slip under NATO's threshold of perception and reaction." Quoted in Mike Collier with Mary Sibierski, "NATO Allies Come to Grips with Russia's 'Hybrid Warfare'" AFP, March 18, 2015.

[3] Interviews with Estonian and Latvian defense officials, Riga and Tallinn, July 2015.

[4] Damien Van Puyvelde, "Hybrid War, Does It Even Exist," *NATO Review*, 2015.

I find that the most significant threat from Russia to the Baltics lies in Russia's conventional forces, not its capacity for irregular warfare or political subversion. I divide potential Russian aggression in the Baltics into three distinct categories of scenarios: nonviolent subversion, covert violent actions, and conventional warfare supported by political subversion. I find that the Baltic countries are not especially vulnerable to nonviolent or covert violent actions by Russia. Given the loyalty of many Russian speakers in the Baltics to their home countries, and their greater economic well-being within the EU, Russia will have difficulty provoking large-scale protests or separatist movements. Covert violent Russian actions are also unlikely to succeed, given preparations in these countries to deploy security forces sufficient to either defeat Russian covert forces or compel Russia to escalate to conventional war. A large-scale conventional Russian incursion into the Baltics would almost inevitably be hybrid in the sense that it would include some effort at political subversion. Nevertheless, the danger of such an attack lies in NATO's local conventional inferiority, not in Russian propaganda or proxy warfare, and as such NATO needs to establish a more credible conventional deterrent.

The limited vulnerability to irregular warfare does not mean that a U.S. or NATO policy can focus exclusively on conventional warfare in deterring or defeating Russian aggression. Effective defense of the Baltics depends on reducing vulnerabilities to all forms of Russian aggression. The greater the perceived vulnerabilities of the Baltic countries to a particular form of aggression, the more likely that Russia is to undertake it. Even if the objective risk of success is limited, Russia could miscalculate or determine that the possible benefit is great enough that risk is justified. Alternatively, war or conflict could emerge by accident. Russia and NATO forces could unintentionally come into conflict, as they did when Turkish forces shot down a Russian plane in November 2015. Or, Russia could become involved if groups allied with the Russian state, but not controlled by them, engage in aggressive action.[5] The failure of Russian-backed armed groups could lead Russia to escalate to avoid defeat, a cycle which could lead to large-scale conflict and even nuclear use. Hence, even if Russia prefers to avoid conflict, a crisis could nevertheless emerge. Strengthening the overall resilience of the Baltic States can reduce the risk of low-level aggression and unintentional escalation.

I conclude this report by suggesting several implications for U.S. and NATO policies to limit the potential for Russian hybrid aggression. First, with regard to nonviolent subversion, pressure from Western allies to improve language and citizenship rights for Russians in the Baltics is probably impractical. Instead, the United States and NATO should pursue the development of a more sophisticated and subtle strategic communication campaign, starting with supporting local Russian-language broadcasters within the Baltic countries.

Second, with regard to covert violent action, continued support for the Baltic countries' security forces is clearly beneficial. The U.S. Air Force can help improve the intelligence, surveillance, and reconnaissance capabilities of the Baltic states by strengthening their technical

---

[5] I am grateful to Paul Stronski for this point.

capabilities for border control and air and maritime domain awareness. NATO and its member states can also do more to share intelligence of Russian policies and actions and help conduct whole-of-government exercises to better prepare for covert or denied Russian aggression. Additional research would also be beneficial to develop and evaluate responses to a wide range of Russian covert tactics.

Third, in developing a credible conventional deterrent in the Baltics, the United States and NATO should attempt to reduce the risk of low-intensity conflict. While there is no way to definitively prevent Russia or Russian speakers in the region from misperceiving NATO's intent, the United States and NATO may be able to deploy forces in a way that would reduce the risk of Russian aggression or subversion. Such actions may include avoiding basing forces in areas dominated by Russian speakers, increasing transparency, limiting activities that appear intended to achieve regime change in Russia, and developing a comprehensive public relations campaign aimed at the Baltic Russian speakers.

# 2. What Is Hybrid Warfare?

The term *hybrid warfare* has no consistent definition and is used by Western analysts and officials in different ways. Some use the term to refer just to irregular tactics, others use *hybrid* to describe a range of irregular and conventional tactics used in the same battlespace, and others use the term to describe the New Generation Warfare doctrine articulated by the senior leadership in the Russian General Staff.[1] Some criticize the term as a meaningless buzzword or catchall that does little to help us understand the specific nature of the threat from Russia.[2] Nevertheless, the various writings on hybrid warfare and associated activities appear to have in mind a similar set of activities that Russia has pursued in Ukraine, Georgia, and other neighboring countries and may be likely to pursue in the future.

These activities, and hence the term *hybrid warfare*, are best described as covert or deniable activities, supported by conventional or nuclear forces, to influence the domestic politics of target countries. By emphasizing that hybrid warfare influences domestic politics, this definition highlights the role of the population in the target state in resisting or responding to Russian activities.[3] Hybrid warfare can be understood as "hybrid" in the sense that Russian activities involve a *combination* of different tactics: conventional forces may be used to shield, support, or defend irregular forces; Russia may use its nuclear forces to deter a response; or Russia's security services and propaganda apparatus may seek to legitimize military action by conventional forces.[4] Defining hybrid warfare as a combination of conventional and irregular means to achieve political objectives, following Frank Hoffman's definition,[5] does not

---

[1] See, respectively, Peter Pindják, "Deterring Hybrid Warfare: A Chance for NATO and the EU to Work Together?" *NATO Review*, 2014; Frank Hoffman, "On Not-So-New Warfare: Political Warfare vs. Hybrid Threats," *War on the Rocks*, July 28, 2014; Mark Galeotti, "The 'Gerasimov Doctrine' and Russian Non-Linear War," *In Moscow's Shadow* (blog), July 6, 2014.

[2] Van Puyvelde, 2015.

[3] A 2015 NATO Parliamentary Assembly publication defined hybrid threats as "the use of asymmetrical tactics to probe for and exploit domestic weaknesses via nonmilitary means, backed by the threat of conventional military means" (NATO Parliamentary Assembly Defence and Security Committee, "Hybrid Warfare: NATO's New Strategic Challenge?" Draft Report, April 7, 2015, p. 3). This recognizes the domestic target of hybrid activities but fails to take into account how the use, and not only the deterrent value, of conventional forces may play an important role in the effectiveness of Russian activities.

[4] As one NATO official noted, Putin "is willing to burn his own house down." Interview with NATO official, Mons, June 17, 2015.

[5] Frank Hoffman, who appears to be the originator of the terms *hybrid warfare* and *hybrid threats*, uses a definition of *hybrid threats* that emphasizes the combination of tactics: "Any adversary that simultaneously employs a tailored mix of conventional weapons, irregular tactics, terrorism, and criminal behavior in the same time and battlespace to obtain their political objectives" (Hoffman, 2014). Similarly, Nadia Schadlow writes, "Hybrid warfare is a term that sought to capture the blurring and blending of previously separate categories of conflict. It uses a blend of military, economic, diplomatic, criminal, and informational means to achieve desired political goals" (Schadlow, 2015).

necessarily distinguish Russian activities in Ukraine or the Baltics from statecraft or warfare more generally. Rather, activities under hybrid warfare are distinct because they are not admitted as official policy, and they primarily seek to influence domestic politics rather than target the armed forces of a given country.[6] Given these characteristics, hybrid warfare may require substantially different responses than other military threats—for example, placing a greater priority on increasing the resilience of the targeted societies to political subversion.

Whatever term is used for Russia's activities, it is imperative to describe the threat concretely in order to analyze its threat to the United States and its allies. There are a wide range of activities and tactics that could be covered under the above definition of hybrid warfare, including cyber warfare, propaganda, proxy warfare (meaning use of third-party, nonstate actors), and a conventional invasion backed by political subversion. In the next section, I disaggregate the "hybrid" threat in the Baltics into different categories of scenarios. Identifying combinations of tactics with different characteristics makes it more feasible to evaluate the vulnerabilities to Russian activities, the responses by the target country, and how the United States and NATO may respond. The analytic lens of the paper thus focuses on the discrete ranges of tactics under the overall category of hybrid warfare, rather than on the meaning, content, and utility of the term *hybrid warfare*.

Still, it is valuable to outline competing ideas about what hybrid warfare consists of, and, drawing from Ukraine, how to understand the threat from Russia short of conventional war. One common understanding of the term *hybrid* is to describe exclusively the irregular tactics used by Russia to influence and subvert the population. A *NATO Review* article, for example, states that "hybrid conflicts involve multilayered efforts designed to destabilize a functioning state and polarize its society."[7] When asked, German and Ukrainian military officers in interviews in mid-2015 defined the hybrid threat as propaganda, support for insurgents, and other subversive activities.[8] However, Russia has not relied solely on irregular warfare in its actions in Ukraine, Georgia, or other neighboring countries to date. Any "hybrid" offensive against the Baltics would similarly likely depend on presence of conventional forces across the border in Russia or deployed in the Baltic states.

---

[6] There are other terms that could be used to describe these activities, such as *political warfare*. Indeed, there may be a sense of conceptual drift from the original use of *hybrid* to refer to conflicts in which state, nonstate, and criminal actors were engaged, or to the use of state capabilities by nonstate actors, as in the 2006 war in Lebanon. Hoffman, for example, writes that hybrid warfare

> blend[s] the lethality of state conflict with the fanatical and protracted fervor of irregular warfare . . . future adversaries (states, state-sponsored groups, or self-funded actors) exploit access to modern military capabilities including encrypted command systems, man-portable surface-to-air missiles, and other modern lethal systems, as well as promote protracted insurgencies that employ ambushes, improvised explosive devices, and assassinations. (Frank Hoffman, "Hybrid Warfare and Challenges," *Joint Forces Quarterly*, Vol. 52, No. 1, January 2009, p. 34)

[7] Pindják, 2014.

[8] Discussions with German and Ukrainian officers, Berlin and Kramatorsk, May and July 2015.

The record of Russian actions in Crimea and eastern Ukraine highlights how the use of irregular activities alone were largely unsuccessful, and shows that Russian success depended on employing superior conventional forces. In Crimea, Russia initiated a large exercise on February 26 and 27, 2014, that served as the launching point and cover for unmarked Russian forces to seize strategic points in the Crimean peninsula.[9] Russia initially denied the presence of its military forces, while Russian propaganda paradoxically sought to legitimize Russian military actions.[10] While Russian propaganda and the use of unmarked forces created a challenge for Western countries to initially attribute responsibility, the presence of large numbers of Russian conventional forces in the region no doubt also helped to deter a strong Western response.[11]

In eastern Ukraine, Russia used irregular warfare to develop the separatist movement, but had to use conventional forces in support of irregular tactics to ensure that the movement was not defeated by Ukrainian forces in August 2014.[12] After protests in Maidan Square in Kyiv forced President Viktor Yanukovych from office in February 2014, Russia appears to have opportunistically coopted an anti-Maidan protest movement that been started by Yanukovych's supporters.[13] Polls in early 2014 indicated little desire in eastern Ukraine for separatism.[14] There is an indication that the anti-Maidan movement only adopted the goal of separatism in the spring of 2014 with the urging of individuals with ties to Russian oligarchs Aleksandr Borodai and Igor Girkin, the latter of whom is commonly known as Strelkov.[15]

Ukrainian forces had difficulty responding to the nascent separatist movement—regular military forces simply could not deploy in response to the government's orders due to limited

---

[9] Martin Hurt, *Lessons Identified in Crimea: Does Estonia's National Defence Model Meet Our Needs?* Tallinn, Estonia: International Centre for Defence and Security, April 2014, p. 1.

[10] Russian propaganda offered messages including the illegitimacy of the post-Maidan government in Kyiv, a threat from fascist elements to the Russian population in Crimea, a threat to the Black Sea fleet, and that there was an invitation from the legitimate government for Russian presence. See Roy Allison, "Russian 'Deniable' Intervention in Ukraine: How and Why Russia Broke the Rules," *International Affairs*, Vol. 90, No. 6, November 2014, pp. 1255–1268.

[11] As the International Institute for Strategic Studies notes, "Russian forces demonstrated integrated use of rapid deployment, electronic warfare, information operations, locally based naval infantry, airborne assault and special-forces capabilities, as well as wider use of cyberspace and strategic communications." International Institute for Strategic Studies, *The Military Balance*, 2015, p. 6. See also Michael Kofman and Matthew Rojansky, "A Closer Look at Russia's 'Hybrid War,'" Woodrow Wilson Center Kennan Cable No. 7, April 2015.

[12] See Samuel Charap, "Ghosts of Hybrid War," *Survival*, Vol. 57, No. 6, December 2015–January 2016, pp. 54–55.

[13] Andrew Roth, "From Russia, 'Tourists' Stir the Protests," *New York Times*, March 3, 2014; Serhiy Kudelia, "Domestic Sources of the Donbas Insurgency," PONARS Eurasia Policy Memo, September 2014; Yuri M. Zhukov, "Rust Belt Rebellion: The Economics Behind Eastern Ukraine's Upheaval," *Foreign Affairs*, Vol. 93, No. 3, June 2014.

[14] Steven Pifer and Hannah Thoburn, "Nuanced Views in Eastern Ukraine," *Brookings*, April 28, 2014.

[15] See Alec Luhn, "Fight Club, Donetsk," *Foreign Policy,* June 16, 2014; Courtney Weaver, "Malofeev: The Russian Billionaire Linking Moscow to the Rebels," *Financial Times,* July 24, 2014; Maksym Bugriy, "Konstantin Malofeev: Fringe Christian Orthodox Financier of the Donbas Separatists," The Jamestown Foundation, August 8, 2014; discussions with U.S. think tank analysts and Ukrainian officials, July 2015 and November 2015.

training, under-investment, embedded corruption, and refusal to see Russia as an enemy.[16] Russia may also have intended for its large conventional presence on the Russian border to deter a Ukrainian attack. These forces do not appear to have actually deterred Ukrainian forces. On July 1, 2014, newly elected Ukrainian President Petro Poroshenko announced a new offensive, stating, "We will attack and liberate our land."[17] Ukrainian mobilization efforts improved the strength of their forces, and Ukraine began to take back significant territory.[18] With the separatist movement on the verge of defeat in mid-August 2014, Russia responded with more-conventional tactics, including firing artillery from its side of the border, increasing its delivery of heavy weapons to the separatists, and sending Russian military forces over the border.[19] Since August 2014, Russia has embedded advisors in separatist formations, and support from regular, albeit unmarked, Russian forces appears critical for the strength of the separatist forces in eastern Ukraine.[20]

In short, the use of irregular tactics on their own in eastern Ukraine was not especially successful, even with the deterrent threat of Russian forces over the border. Even the relatively weak post-Maidan government was able to defeat the separatists, likely in part due to its ability to deploy sizable formations that could control Ukrainian territory. The use of Russian conventional forces in combination with irregular warfare—including propaganda, support for

---

[16] One Ukrainian officer observed that the troops were unprepared to even drive over a field of newly planted wheat in the spring of 2014, much less to actually fight the separatists. Only the newly created National Guard was able to mobilize significant troops (interviews with Ukrainian officers, Kyiv, April and May 2015). See also J. C. Finley, "Ukrainian President Announces Creation of National Guard, Mobilization of Armed Forces," UPI, March 11, 2014; Anthony Faiola, "Ukraine Mobilizes Reservists but Relies on Diplomacy," *Washington Post*, March 17, 2014.

[17] "Address of President of Ukraine Petro Poroshenko," July 1, 2014.

[18] Michael Kofman argues that Russian tactics in the early summer took on a "hybrid" character, as they included both irregular and conventional elements:

> It was only at the end of May, when irregular warfare had run into too much resistance from Ukraine's volunteer battalions and armed forces, that we began to see Russia backing into a hybridized approach. Here I'm referencing the introduction of high-end conventional capabilities, and the intermixing of Russian units along with individual Russian soldiers among the separatist force. We should keep in mind that this was Russia's third attempt to get the Ukrainian leadership to concede to its political demands. (Kofman, "Russian Hybrid Warfare and Other Dark Arts," *War on the Rocks*, March 11, 2016)

[19] Igor Sutyagin writes,

> The first phase of large-scale incursions by regular Russian troops commenced on 11 August 2014 and has involved a substantial array of forces. Elements of some Russian reconnaissance and special operations units have operated on Ukrainian soil since 14 July (at the latest), comprising teams generated by six units. (Sutyagin, "Russian Forces in Ukraine," RUSI Briefing paper, March 2015, p. 1)

See also Charap, 2015–2016, pp. 55–56; David Herszenhorn and Peter Baker, "Russia Steps Up Help for Rebels in Ukraine War," *New York Times*, July 25, 2014; NATO, "New Satellite Imagery Exposes Russian Combat Troops Inside Ukraine," August 28, 2014.

[20] Interviews with Ukrainian officers, Kyiv and Kramatorsk, May 2015. See International Crisis Group, "The Ukraine Crisis: Risks of Renewed Military Conflict After Minsk II," Crisis Group Europe Briefing No. 73, April 1, 2015; Sutyagin, 2015.

the separatists as proxies, and covert action—does appear to have had some success in creating a difficult-to-resolve frozen conflict in eastern Ukraine. If the concept of hybrid warfare does not include conventional warfare, the term fails to adequately describe Russian military action in eastern Ukraine, or to characterize potential, comparable Russian actions in the Baltics.

Other analysts have described Russian hybrid warfare based on the Russian concept of New Generation Warfare. As Dima Adamsky explains, New Generation Warfare "is an amalgamation of hard and soft power across various domains, through skillful application of coordinated military, diplomatic, and economic tools."[21] A February 2013 article by Chief of the General Staff in Russia, General Valery Gerasimov, is commonly cited as a clear articulation of New Generation Warfare, and an example of Russian thinking about hybrid warfare.[22] Gerasimov writes,

> The very "rules of war" have changed. The role of non-military means of achieving political and strategic goals has grown, and, in many cases, they have exceeded the power of force of weapons in their effectiveness. . . . The focus of applied methods of conflict has altered in the direction of the broad use of political, economic, informational, humanitarian, and other non-military measures—applied in coordination with the protest potential of the population.[23]

Indeed, analysts have identified a "Gerasimov doctrine" and begun to associate his thinking with hybrid warfare.[24] While hybrid warfare, in the sense of a combination of activities to influence domestic politics, is part of New Generation Warfare, Russian authors writing on New Generation Warfare are also focused on changes in the conventional battlespace, especially the impact of the growing use of high-precision weapons.[25]

---

[21] Dmitry (Dima) Adamsky, "Cross-Domain Coercion: The Current Russian Art of Strategy," Institut Français des Relations Internationales, November 2015, pp. 21–23. However, Adamsky is critical of using the Western lens of "hybrid warfare" to understand Russian thinking or behavior.

[22] Coalson, 2014; Galeotti, 2014.

[23] Quoted in Coalson, 2014.

[24] See Galeotti, 2014; Sam Jones, "Ukraine: Russia's New Art of War," *Financial Times*, August 28, 2014. A U.S. Army Special Operations Command white paper observes, citing the Gerasimov paper,

> Russian UW is thus the central, most game-changing component of a Hybrid Warfare effort involving conventional forces, economic intimidation of regional countries, influence operations, force-posturing all along NATO borders, and diplomatic intervention. Sponsorship of separatist insurgency in Ukraine accords well with current Russian military doctrine and strategy, which embrace "asymmetrical actions . . . [including] special-operations forces and internal opposition to create a permanently operating front through the entire territory of the enemy state." (U.S. Army Special Operations Command, "Counter-Unconventional Warfare White Paper," September 26, 2014, p. 4.)

[25] According to Sergei Chekinov and Sergei Bogdanov's account, just the "opening period [of a New Generation War] . . . will break down into a targeted information operation . . . the use of high-precision weapons launched from various platforms; long range artillery, [etc.]" (Chekinov and Bogdanov, "The Nature and Content of a New-Generation War," *Military Thought*, Vol. 4., 2013, p. 21).

Aside from Western definitions of hybrid warfare, recent Russian strategy doctrines, including the 2015 military doctrine[26] and national security strategy[27] emphasize the use of combinations of different tactics, irregular warfare, and political subversion. This emphasis draws from a long history of Russian military thought on the use of irregular forces, influence operations, and deception (*maskirovka*). As Jānis Bērziņš writes,

> The Russians have placed the idea of influence at the very center of their operational planning and used all possible levers to achieve this: the skillful internal communications; deception operations; psychological operations and well-constructed external communications.[28]

Further, subversion and domestic influence also draw on the use of "political technologies"—manipulation of political outcomes through deception or manipulation—in Russia's domestic politics.[29]

A range of works have criticized the use of the term *hybrid*, or its utility in understanding Russian activities. Some question the value of focusing on the irregular elements of hybrid warfare, drawing on the questionable performance of Russian "hybrid" warfare in Ukraine. Ruslan Pukhov, a Russian think-tank director, writes in the *Moscow Times*, "It is not difficult to see that these definitions of hybrid war, and especially the characterization of Russia's actions in 2014 as such, are out of touch with reality."[30] Pukhov notes that Russia had a "sluggish propaganda campaign" in Crimea, and observes that any effort to capture a territory will involve irregular activities included under the term hybrid warfare.[31] Indeed, Russian propaganda was not universally persuasive in eastern Ukraine—for example, support for Russia's agenda was

---

[26] Olga Oliker, "Russia's New Military Doctrine: Same as the Old Doctrine, Mostly," *Washington Post*, January 15, 2015.

[27] The strategy notes,

> Interrelated political, military, military-technical, diplomatic, economic, informational, and other measures are being developed and implemented in order to ensure strategic deterrence and the prevention of armed conflicts. These measures are intended to prevent the use of armed force against Russia, and to protect its sovereignty and territorial integrity. (Russian Federation, "On the Russian Federation's National Security Strategy," December 31, 2015, para 36, copy with author)

[28] Jānis Bērziņš, "Russia's New Generation Warfare in Ukraine: Implications for Latvian Defense Policy," National Defence Academy of Latvia, Center for Security and Strategic Research, Policy Paper No. 2, April 2014, p. 6.

[29] See, among others, Merle Maigre, "Nothing New in Hybrid Warfare: The Estonian Experience and Recommendations for NATO," German Marshall Fund of the United States, February 2015, p. 2; Andrew Wilson, *Virtual Politics: Faking Democracy in the Post-Soviet World*, New Haven, Conn.: Yale University Press, 2005.

[30] Ruslan Pukhov, "Nothing 'Hybrid' About Russia's War in Ukraine," *The Moscow Times*, May 27, 2015. Pukhov quotes the International Institute for Strategic Studies' definition of

> the use of military and non-military tools in an integrated campaign designed to achieve surprise, seize the initiative and gain psychological as well as physical advantages utilizing diplomatic means; sophisticated and rapid information, electronic and cyber operations; covert and occasionally overt military and intelligence action; and economic pressure. (International Institute for Strategic Studies, 2015, p. 17)

[31] Pukhov, 2015.

dramatically higher in Crimea than in the surrounding oblasts with similar linguistic characteristics.[32]

There is also an argument that Moscow has paid high costs for its operation in eastern Ukraine that may lead Russian policymakers to question repeating a similar campaign.[33] Estonian and Latvian officials, as well as Western analysts, similarly observe that it is unlikely that Russia will repeat the same tactics again.[34] Samuel Charap also writes "there is no evidence to suggest the emergence of a hybrid-war doctrine" and notes that the campaign in Ukraine was limited and in a relatively unique context.[35] There are also questions about how directly Russia is in control of events in eastern Ukraine, given reports of assassinations of separatist leaders and competition between the Russian security services. Strelkov, for example, was removed from the leadership of the separatist movement, escorted back to Moscow, and subsequently became a critic of Russia's policy by urging a more aggressive approach in Ukraine.[36] The principal-agent problems between Russia and its proxies in Ukraine would likely reoccur in future operations.

A second criticism of Russia's use of hybrid warfare claims that Russian military officials are making observations about the U.S. threat, rather than describing Russian activities. Charap writes, "Gerasimov is actually describing what he sees as the new US way of war, not Russian doctrine."[37] Olga Oliker similarly writes on Russia's new doctrine,

> While Western readers might immediately see aspects of [the focus on information warfare and political warfare] as strikingly descriptive of Russia's activities in Ukraine (and the Western debate on so-called "hybrid" warfare), from Moscow's perspective, these are threats to Russia.[38]

Discussions by the Russian General Staff, including Gerasimov, at public events also emphasizes the perception that Russia is threatened by Western ability to use combinations of military and

---

[32] John O'Loughlin and Gerard Toal, "Mistrust About Political Motives in Contested Ukraine," *Washington Post*, February 13, 2015.

[33] See, for example, Boris Nemtsov's report identifying approximately 220 Russian casualties in Ukraine, and Moscow's subsequent efforts to silence information about Russian casualties. Courtney Weaver, "Nemtsov's Final Report Says 220 Russian Troops Have Died in Ukraine," *Financial Times*, May 12, 2015; Kathrin Hille, "Russia Censors Discussion of Involvement in Ukraine," *Financial Times*, May 28, 2015.

[34] Interviews and discussions with Estonian and Latvian defense officials and Western analysts, Tallinn, Riga, and Washington D.C., July 2015, November 2015, and January 2016.

[35] Charap, 2015–2016, pp. 53–55.

[36] Discussions with an academic expert and Ukrainian officials, April 2015 and January 2016; Stepan Kravchenko "The Rebel Leader Who Makes Putin Look Cautious," *Bloomberg,* February 4, 2015; Andrew Roth, "Former Russian Rebels Trade War in Ukraine for Posh Life in Moscow," *Washington Post,* September 16, 2015.

[37] Charap, 2015–2016, p. 53.

[38] See Oliker, 2015. Similarly, Kofman and Rojansky (2015) note

> Rather than a genuine strategic concept built from the ground up by the Russians themselves, "hybrid war" is merely a label attributed to Russian actions in Ukraine by the West, in an effort to make sense of cascading phases of a security crisis in which all sides but Russia seem to have been caught off balance.

nonmilitary tactics to influence Russia's domestic politics.[39] It may make the most sense to view statements by Gerasimov and others as identifying changes in the nature of warfare, with a focus on *both* identifying the threat to Russia and considering how to adapt Russia's capabilities to meet this new threat in kind.[40]

While the concept of hybrid warfare is contested, it remains a useful framework to understand a potential Russian threat in the Baltics. Russian officials are clearly thinking about how to combine deniable or covert activities with other military tools to achieve their political objectives. Events in Ukraine offer a useful set of examples of how Russia may engage hybrid warfare in practice. For example, accounts of Ukraine show how the use of proxies and propaganda is not universally effective, coordination across the government is inconsistent (though improving),[41] and irregular forces may need to call on conventional support. Russian tactics in the Ukraine may differ substantially from those used in the Baltics. Hence, it is critical to understand concretely what forms Russian aggression may take and the vulnerability of the Baltic states to different scenarios.

---

[39] Dmitry Gorenberg paraphrases Gerasimov, arguing

> that the U.S. can't deal with more equal relations among states, so it is using new tactics to assure its supremacy . . . the United States has developed a new method of warfare, beginning with using non-military tactics to change opposing governments through colored revolutions that utilize the protest potential of the population to engineer peaceful regime change. (Dmitry Gorenburg, "Moscow Conference on International Security 2015, Part 2: Gerasimov on Military Threats Facing Russia," *Russian Military Reform*, May 4, 2015)

[40] Adamsky (2015, p. 42), for example, assesses Russian activities in Syria as following the pattern of Russia attempting to respond to a Western hybrid threat in kind:

> As the contours of Russian campaign design are slowly emerging, one may assume that it may also draw from the NGW [New Generation Warfare] concept. . . . Moscow perceived the situation in Syria as the result of a U.S. effort, albeit one which failed to conduct HW [hybrid warfare] against the incumbent regime along the lines of the Libyan scenario. Moscow's demarche, although driven by the interplay of several factors, was a countermeasure to such a perceived U.S. effort, but was shaped along similar operational lines.

[41] Charap (2015–2016, p. 53) writes, "Russian actions in Ukraine did demonstrate important new developments. Most significantly, Moscow coordinated the arms of national power effectively in order to achieve its objectives." For example, the National Center for the Management of Defense is a new "interagency nerve centre that came online in early 2014."

# 3. Hybrid Scenarios

I identify three categories of hybrid scenarios in the Baltics: nonviolent subversion, which seeks to use propaganda, covert action, and other nonviolent means to undermine or influence the governments of the Baltic states; covert violent action, in which Russia would use armed force in an nonattributable or deniable manner; and conventional aggression supported and legitimized by a range of propaganda, covert action, and other forms of irregular warfare. These three categories seek to include the scenarios proposed by officials and analysts in the United States, Baltics, and other NATO countries, and to cover the range of possible Russian actions.

Analysts outside of the Baltic countries generally agree that low-level nonviolent subversion is currently happening and could intensify in the future, although it will pose limited danger of destabilization; that covert violent action is unlikely but possible, and could divide NATO; and that conventional aggression is very unlikely, although it would be very dangerous if it were to occur. Baltic officials agree that nonviolent subversion is ongoing and likely but poses limited risk, generally downplay their vulnerability to Russian covert violent action, and highlight the need to take seriously a large-scale conventional attack.[1] Baltic officials' view of Russia and the potential for subversion is likely influenced both by their proximity to Russia, and hence their greater awareness of the threat it might pose, as well as their efforts to develop the independence and national identity of their own states. Baltic officials may tend to downplay the dissatisfaction of and risk of subversion by Russian speakers to imply that their efforts at integration are more effective, and that the states based on the identity of the titular group (i.e., Estonian, Latvian, or Lithuanian) are sustainable.[2]

The division of scenarios into three categories is not meant to imply that Russian activities would necessary be limited to a single category during a particular crisis or series of events. Russia could easily decide to escalate to covert violent action or conventional attack if its efforts at nonviolent subversion are not successful. Analyzing each type of Russian aggression makes it possible to better understand vulnerabilities and formulate appropriate responses. Together, these responses can be integrated into an overall policy for defense and deterrence.

---

[1] Interviews with NATO, Polish, Baltic, and U.S. officials; Brussels, Mons, Warsaw, Riga, Tallinn; June and July 2015.

[2] Andres Kasekamp, *A History of the Baltics*, New York: Plagrave Macmillan, 2010, pp. 184–191; David Laitin, *Identity in Formation*, Ithaca, N.Y.: Cornell University Press, 1998, pp. 93–98; discussion with Baltic officials and U.S. think tank analysts, June, July, and December 2015.

## Nonviolent Subversion

According to officials in the Baltic countries, they have been under attack for decades by Russian propaganda, cyber attacks, and other nonviolent means of subversion.[3] Russia likely seeks some measure of control over the decisions of its neighbors and hopes to undermine EU and NATO expansion, while at the same time avoiding the potential for military conflict with NATO.[4] To these ends, Russia may seek to gain influence over the internal politics of the Baltic countries, to provoke internal instability, or to engineer the takeover of the legitimately elected government by factions loyal to Moscow, while denying its role in any such activities.

Estonia and Latvia are the most vulnerable to Russian subversion due to their large Russian-speaking minorities (Figure 3.1). The majority of Russian speakers came to Estonia and Latvia during the Soviet era, thanks to policies intended to dilute the dominance of the majority ethnic group in these countries.[5] Lithuania did not experience significant in-migration of Russian speakers, and thus by 2011 had only 8 percent Russian speakers (including Ukrainian, Belarussian, and other nationalities whose primary language was Russian and whose preferences tend to align with the Russian minority),[6] of which 6 percent were ethnic Russians. By comparison, in 2011 Estonia had 30 percent Russian speakers, of which 25 percent are ethnic Russians,[7] and Latvia had approximately 35 percent Russian speakers of which 27 percent were ethnic Russians.[8] Given the larger proportion and influence of the Russian minorities in Estonia and Latvia compared with Lithuania, I focus on the threat of Russian subversion in Estonia and Latvia, although many in Lithuania are certainly concerned about Russian influence in their country.[9]

---

[3] Interview with Baltic defense officials, Riga and Tallinn, July 2015.

[4] Olga Oliker, Keith Crane, Lowell H. Schwartz, and Catherine Yusupov, *Russian Foreign Policy: Sources and Implications*, Santa Monica, Calif.: RAND Corporation, MG-768-AF, 2009, pp. 93–95; Mike Winnerstig, ed., *Tools of Destabilization: Russian Soft Power and Non-Military Influence in the Baltic States*, Sweden Defense Research Agency (FOI), December 2014, pp. 18–20; S. R. Covington, *Putin's Choice for Russia*, Cambridge, Mass.: Harvard Kennedy School, Belfer Center for Science and International Affairs, August 2015.

[5] The proportion of the titular group as a percentage of the population went from 94 percent in Estonia and 80 percent in Latvia in 1945 to 62 percent in Estonia and 52 percent in Latvia in 1989. See Kasekamp, 2010, p. 155.

[6] See among others Laitin, 1998, Chapter 10.

[7] The proportion of Russian speakers in Estonia is based on who identify their "mother tongue" as Russian, see Statistical Office of Estonia, Central Statistical Bureau of Latvia, and Statistics Lithuania, "2011 Population and Housing Censuses in Estonia, Latvia, and Lithuania," 2015, pp. 12, 24.

[8] The proportion of Russian speakers in Latvia is based on comparing the population of Russians, Belarusians, Ukrainians, and Poles relative to overall population of Latvia, because a similar question of mother tongue does not appear to have been asked. See Statistical Office of Estonia, Central Statistical Bureau of Latvia, and Statistics Lithuania, 2015, p. 24. Agnia Grigas observes 34 percent Russian speakers in Latvia (Agnia Grigas, "The New Generation of Baltic Russian Speakers," EurActiv.com, November 28, 2014.)

[9] See, e.g., Winnerstig, 2014, Chapter 5.

**Figure 3.1. Concentrations of Russian Speakers in Estonia and Latvia**

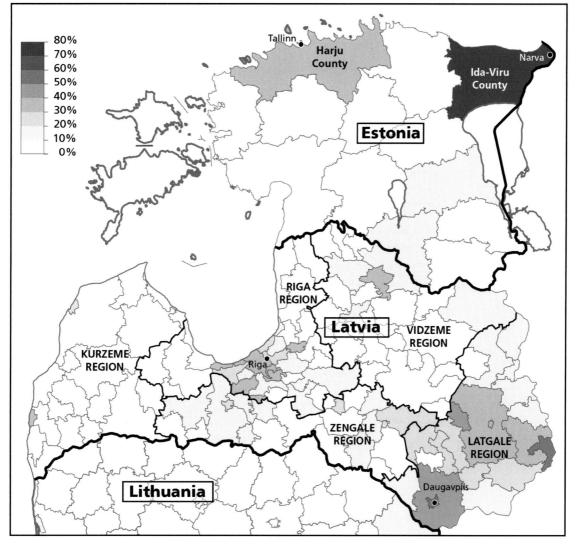

SOURCE: Adapted from Xil, "Russians in Baltic States (2011)," no date.
RAND *RR1577-3.1*

With the collapse of the Soviet Union, the newly independent Baltic States sought to establish a clear identity in line with their own language and nationality.[10] Estonia and Latvia adopted a policy of legal continuity with the pre–World War II governments, which meant that individuals who could not trace their ancestry in Estonia or Latvia to before 1940 had to apply for naturalization. The key requirement for naturalization became a language exam, which effectively disenfranchised the Russian-speaking population who could not or would not pass an exam in the titular language. Russian speakers who did not become citizens of Estonia or Latvia fell into two general categories—Russian citizens (6.8 percent of the total population of Estonia

---

[10] See, inter alia, Mikko Lagerspetz, "Cultural Autonomy of National Minorities in Estonia: The Erosion of a Promise," *Journal of Baltic Studies*, Vol. 45, No. 4, 2014, pp. 457–475.

and 2.1 percent in Latvia in 2015)[11] and stateless individuals who were eventually issued aliens' passports that permitted visa-free travel and work throughout the EU (6.2 percent in Estonia and 12.2 percent in Latvia in 2015).[12] The negotiations surrounding EU accession in 2004 as well as subsequent decisions have led to significant improvement in integration efforts of these populations, including easing the process of naturalization for the children of noncitizens and introducing Estonian or Latvian language education in Russian-language schools.[13] Nevertheless, there remains a perception of discrimination, especially in Estonia.[14] One possible further step would be to recognize Russian as an official language, thereby facilitating relations between these minorities and the state. However, leaders in both countries fear that official recognition of the Russian language would compromise the usage of the titular language and hence the survival of Estonia and Latvia as independent countries, in addition to undermining efforts to integrate Russian speakers.[15]

Russian speakers in Estonia and Latvia are concentrated mainly in the major cities or in Russian-dominated regions. Within Estonia, 87 percent of ethnic Russians live in two counties: Harju, which contains Tallinn, and Ida-Viru, in the northeast of Estonia.[16] In Latvia, 70 percent live in Riga or Latgale regions.[17] While Russians living in both capital cities tend to be relatively better off economically, those in rural areas face substantially higher unemployment and are more likely to be in the lowest income brackets (according to the 2011 census, unemployment in Estonia as a whole was 5.3 percent, compared with 8.3 percent in Ida-Viru county).[18] The gross domestic product (GDP) per capita of the key Russian majority regions of Estonia and Latvia are somewhat higher than the neighboring regions in Russia, especially for Latvia (per capita GDP in 2013 was $12,975 in Ida-Viru in Estonia, compared with $11,886 in the neighboring

---

[11] The number of Russian citizens may have increased due to Russian efforts to give citizenship to Russian speakers with indeterminate citizenship. See Winnerstig, 2014, p. 36.

[12] Estonia.eu, "Citizenship," August 10, 2015; Central Statistics Bureau of Latvia, 2015 data.

[13] See Kasekamp, 2010, pp. 185–186; Latvijas Republikas Saeima, "Saeima Adopts Provisions on Recognition of Dual Citizenship." May 9, 2013; "Riigikogu Simplifies Granting Estonian Citizenship to Children and Elderly," *The Baltic Course*, January 22, 2015. On schooling, see also Estonia.eu, "Russian-Language Schools' Transition to Partial Estonian-Language Instruction—What Is Happening and Why?" January 31, 2013.

[14] European Union Agency for Fundamental Rights, *European Union Minorities and Discrimination Survey: Main Results Report*, 2009, p. 178.

[15] One think tank analyst in Riga explained a commonly held view that recognition of the Russian language would lead to the disappearance of Latvian within two generations (interviews with Estonian and Latvian officials and analysts, Riga and Tallinn, July 2015; see also reporting on the 2012 language referendum in Latvia: "What's My Language?" *The Economist*, February 14, 2012; David Herszenhorn "Latvians Reject Russian as Second Language," *New York Times*, February 19, 2012).

[16] Statistical Office of Estonia, Statistics Database, 2015.

[17] Central Statistics Bureau of Latvia, 2014 data.

[18] See Statistical Office of Estonia, 2015, question PC007 (available at http://pub.stat.ee/px-web.2001/Dialog/statfile1.asp); Bertelsmann Stiftung, "BTI 2014—Latvia Country Report," 2014, p. 12.

Leningrad Oblast in Russia, and $7,866 for Latgale in Latvia, compared with $5,227 in the neighboring Pskov Oblast).[19]

Many Russian speakers vote for Russian-dominated parties, which have become some of the largest in Estonia and Latvia. Despite their significant size, these parties have not been part of governing coalitions, as Russian speakers are an underrepresented minority of overall voters,[20] and mainstream Estonian and Latvia parties are wary of considering them as potential partners given fears of Russian influence.[21] While Estonia initially had a political system that did not have clearly Russian parties, the Centre Party, led by Estonian Edgar Savisaar, has come to be perceived as a predominately Russian party, and it had 25 percent of the vote in 2015.[22] In Latvia, Harmony Centre, led by the popular Russian-speaking mayor of Riga, Nils Ushakovs, is the largest political party in the country, with 28 percent of the vote in the 2014 election.[23] Both parties have ties with Russia's ruling party, United Russia.[24]

There is important variation in the level of social, economic, and political integration of the Russian population across Estonia and Latvia, within different regions in each country, and among individuals. Russians in Latvia appear to be somewhat better integrated than those in Estonia—one-third of marriages are interethnic, and 15 percent of those serving in Latvia's armed forces are Russian speakers.[25] Many Russians in Estonia are similarly integrated into Estonian society, participating in the military or high political office. One Estonian think tank study, for example, distinguishes different "clusters" among the Russian population based on their level of linguistic, political, and social integration, from the "successfully" integrated

---

[19] Russia in general also has higher inequality. See Statistical Office of Estonia, 2015; Central Statistics Bureau of Latvia, 2015; Knoema, "Leningrad Region—Gross Regional Product Per Capita," multiple years; Knoema, "Pskov Region—Gross Regional Product Per Capita," multiple years. Exchange rates from Internal Revenue Service, "Yearly Average Currency Exchange Rates," 2016. For inequality data, see World Bank, "GINI index (World Bank Estimate)," 2016.

[20] The percentage of Russians supporting ethnic Russian parties appears to be highly variable—for example, one set of surveys in Estonia revealed 61.5 percent support of Russians for ethnic parties in 2001, and only 35.2 percent in 2004. See Holley Hansen, "Ethnic Voting and Representation: Minority Russians in Post-Soviet States," Ph.D. dissertation, University of Iowa, 2009, p. 167.

[21] See, for example, the recent commentary surrounding the elections in both countries—coalition with a Russian party was not considered a feasible option for the major parties. *The Economist* quotes a Latvia expert, noting, "'Harmony joining any ruling coalition would be breaking two taboos at once. It is Russian speaking and it is a social democratic party.' Both would be a first for post-Soviet Latvia" ("Latvia Election: How to Deal with Harmony," October 5, 2014, *The Economist*). "On the Border," *The Economist*, March 5, 2015; interviews with Latvian and Estonian think tank analysts, July 2015.

[22] Richard Milne, "Party with Ties to Putin Pushes Ahead in Estonian Polls," *Financial Times*, February 27, 2015; BBC, "Estonia's Ruling Party Wins Election Victory," March 2, 2015a.

[23] Licia Cianetti, "The Governing Parties Survived Latvia's Election, but the Issue of the Country's Russian-Speaking Minority Remains Centre-Stage," London School of Economics and Political Science, October 8, 2014.

[24] Milne, 2015; "Latvia's Election: How to Deal with Harmony," 2014.

[25] The high level of integration of Russians makes some Latvians nervous that Latvian language or culture will be overwhelmed by Russian. Interviews with former Latvian government official and analyst, Riga, July 2015.

population (21 percent) to an "'unintegrated' group of mainly older Russian citizens" (22 percent).[26] Journalists note that even Russian speakers who voice support for Vladimir Putin's policies in Ukraine, and hence are presumably the strongest advocates for separatism, nevertheless reject any idea of revolt against the Estonian government.[27]

Russia has sought to maintain a connection to and influence among the Russian speakers in the Baltics. Its Compatriots Policy, for example, funds pro-Russia organizations in the Baltics, supports educational exchanges, and seeks to protect the interests of Russians abroad.[28] While Russia justifies the Compatriots Policy as a legitimate cultural institution, Baltic analysts see this policy as a strategy of impeding the integration of the Russian population, perhaps with the hope of using them in the future to pursue Russia's interests.[29] Russian propaganda, controlled and funded by the state, also has a tremendous influence on Russian speakers in the Baltics. Many observers also note that products on Russian media generally have significantly higher production values than locally produced shows, and that even if Russian speakers do understand the titular language media, Russian television in particular is easier and more enjoyable to watch.[30] Russian speakers therefore exist in a "separate informational space" from the Estonian or Latvian population.[31] Security services in Estonia and Latvia publicly report their concerns about Russia's use of its Compatriots Policy and propaganda as a means of undermining Estonia and Latvia's sovereignty and security, including by promoting alternative views of the Soviet Union's occupation of the Baltics and by convincing the population that the Baltic governments are fascist.[32]

---

[26] Juhan Kivirähk, "Integrating Estonia's Russian-Speaking Population: Findings of National Defense Opinion Surveys," International Centre for Defence and Security, December 2014, pp. 8–9.

[27] One article explains:

> The situation crystallises in a warehouse outside Tallinn, where a volunteer group called Dobrosvet is collecting humanitarian aid for civilians in rebel-held eastern Ukraine. Boxes stuffed with food and clothes lean in precarious stacks, waiting to be sent to hospitals, schools and villages throughout the Donbas. The boxes will travel through Russia with the help of the Night Wolves, a Kremlin-endorsed nationalist biker gang. Yet even these activists, like Mr Ponjatovsky in Narva, call Estonia home. Russians in Estonia "already have a different mentality," says Elina Esakova, Dobrosvet's leader. Her son will serve in Estonia's army. ("On the Border," 2015.)

[28] Winnerstig, 2014, pp. 22–24.

[29] Winnerstig, 2014, p. 114.

[30] Interviews with Baltic officials and analysts, Riga and Tallinn, July 2015.

[31] In Estonia, for example,

> Estonians and non-Estonians live in different information spaces, often with contrasting content. . . . Most of the Russian-speaking population derives its information and views on history and current events from Russian television channels that are directly subordinate to the Kremlin and can be used as a mechanism of propaganda. (Winnerstig, 2014, p. 53)

[32] The Estonian Internal Security Service reports,

> the more active Russian nationalists get support from Russian national funds and agencies and earn their living by spreading the three main messages of Russia's influence operations and fighting against integration between the various ethnic and language groups living in Estonia. The

Russia has historically used proxies, propaganda, cyber attacks, and possibly other means to foment pro-Russian protests and instability in the Baltics. In 2007 in Estonia, riots broke out after the Estonian government announced plans to move a statue commemorating the victory over the Nazis from central Tallinn to a military cemetery. Merle Maigre, an advisor to the President of Estonia, identifies the events surrounding the movement of the statue as an example of "a conflict of a hybrid nature," since it included "riots in Tallinn, a siege of the Estonian Embassy in Moscow by pro-Kremlin Nashi youth organization demonstrators, strong economic measures imposed by Russia against Estonia, waves of cyber-attacks against the Estonian government and banking systems, and a fiery official Russian response."[33] Nevertheless, there is good reason to believe that while Russia may have played a role in encouraging the protests, and certainly supported them, it did not orchestrate the events. Protests by local Russian speakers immediately followed rumors of the movement of the statue.[34] The presence of cyber attacks may appear to indicate a role by the Russian state, but the first phase of the cyber attacks, from April 27 to 29, appears to be "emotionally motivated, as the attacks were relatively simple and any coordination mainly occurred on an ad hoc basis."[35] The intensity and sophistication of the attacks increased significantly with a second wave, from April 30 to May 18.[36] Although preplanning and close coordination by the Russian authorities is impossible to rule out, it seems unlikely given the timing of the observed events.

There are also reports of Russia unsuccessfully testing the potential for protest and separatism in eastern Russian-dominated areas of both countries prior to the conflict in Ukraine.[37] A Russian court has questioned the legitimacy of the independence of the Baltic

---

> three main messages they try to promote are: Estonia supports Nazism; Russian-speaking people are discriminated against in Estonia en masse; Estonia is a dead-end state that only causes problems for its Western partners. (Estonia Internal Security Service, *Annual Report 2013*, p. 5)

The Latvian Security Police similarly notes,

> in 2013, Russia actively used information space in order to spread the information discrediting Latvia. For several years already, the opinion of alleged "rebirth of Fascism and its glorification" and "violation of Russian-speaking rights" in Latvia was intensively spread, at the same time denying occupation of Latvia in 1940. (Latvia Security Police, *Annual Report 2013*, p. 15)

[33] Maigre, 2015, p. 4.

[34] Karsten Brüggemann and Andres Kasekamp, "The Politics of History and the 'War of Monuments' in Estonia," *Nationalities Papers,* Vol. 36, No. 3, July 2008, p. 436; Martin Ehala, "The Bronze Soldier: Identity Threat and Maintenance in Estonia," *Journal of Baltic Studies*, Vol. 40, No. 1, 2009, pp. 142–143, 152–155.

[35] The initial attack was apparently begun when instructions for executing ping commands was posted on various Russian-language Internet forums. One paper explains, "As a generalisation, though, the initial attacks on April 27 and 28 were simple, ineptly coordinated and easily mitigated" (Eneken Tikk, Kadri Kaska, and Liis Vihul, "International Cyber Incidents: Legal Considerations," Tallinn, Estonia: Cooperative Cyber Defence Centre of Excellence [CCD COE], 2010, p. 18).

[36] Tikk, Kaska, and Vihul, 2010, pp. 20–22.

[37] Interviews with Estonian and Latvian officials, Tallinn and Riga, July 2015.

countries in a recent case.[38] There is some evidence that Russian influence and geopolitical instability can shift the opinions, and perhaps behavior, of Russian speakers over time. An Estonian think tank report, for example, links the extensive variation in support for NATO among Russian-speaking Estonians from 2000 to 2014 (between 20 percent and 52 percent) to coverage of political events in the Russian-language media.[39] An additional challenge is the presence of organized criminal networks with links to Russia. Mark Galeotti notes that organized criminal networks in the Baltics likely have ties with Moscow, and can be used "as an instrument to gather intelligence and exert influence abroad."[40]

These demographic and political considerations are believed to enable two general scenarios for subversion. First, Russia may exert influence over one of the Baltic countries through a proxy, such as a predominately Russian political party with close links to Moscow or use of organized criminal networks.

Many Latvian analysts, for example, express concern about Harmony Centre's funding and close ties with Moscow, claiming that the Latvian population would view Harmony's entry into a governing coalition as a security risk.[41] Similarly, in Estonia, concerns have been raised about Russian influence over Savisaar's Centre Party.[42] However, given the fears of the Estonian and Latvian majority about Russian influence, as mentioned above, major parties in both countries are unlikely to go into coalition with any Russian-dominated party.[43] Alternatively, Russia may attempt to work through organized crime or another proxy to exert influence on particular individuals in the government. The exact mechanism is different to specify, as such an activity would necessarily be covert, and the opportunity would depend on the particular individuals involved.

Even if Moscow were to bribe or otherwise influence Estonian or Latvian parties to bring in a Russian party to the coalition or to adjust their policy to support Russian interests, there are real limits on the extent to which an individual or party could counter the overwhelming pro-

---

[38] Ariel Cohen, "Putin Explores Legal Loopholes to Take Back the Baltic Nations," *Newsweek*, July 16, 2015.

[39] Kivirähk, 2014, pp. 15–17.

[40] Mark Galeotti, "Organized Crime in the Baltic States," *Baltic Review,* March 24, 2015. Other sources note money-laundering operations in Latvia, and links between Russian organized crime and Lithuanian politicians. See Lawless Latvia, website, no date; Agnia Grigas, *Beyond Crimea: The New Russian Empire*, New Haven, Conn.: Yale University Press, 2016, p. 162.

[41] Interviews with Latvian analysts, Riga, July 2015.

[42] Leonid Bershidsky, "Estonia Can Handle Putin's Soft Power," *BloombergView*, March 2, 2015.

[43] In November 2016, after the initial drafting of this report, Centre Party joined the governing coalition in Estonia after Savizaar was replaced as the party's leader by Juri Ratas, who became Prime Minister. Though some Estonian parties and Western media sources have noted Centre Party's existing ties with Russia, Ratas has emphasized that Centre Party's agreement with United Russia is "frozen," and the new coalition has stated that it will continue Estonia's foreign policy based on its membership in the EU and NATO (Richard Martyn-Hemphill, "Estonia's New Premier Comes From Party with Links to Russia," *New York Times,* November 20, 2016; "Ratas: Estonian Center Party's Agreement with United Russia Is Non-Active," *Posttimees,* November 10, 2016; Joanna Hyndle-Hussein, "The New Government in Estonia," Center for Eastern Studies (OSW), November 30, 2016).

European and pro-NATO policy consensus in the Baltic countries absent the use of violence. Russia may be far more able to achieve smaller gains on noncore interests—such as increasing the economic influence of Russian companies—than on being able to organize a fundamental shift on policy to reflect Russia's interests on foreign and security policy.

A second commonly raised scenario is the development of a locally organized separatist or protest movement in the Russian-dominated areas of eastern Estonia or Latvia. The town of Narva in Estonia, whose population is composed of more than 90 percent Russian speakers, is often cited as a perhaps the greatest point of vulnerability.[44] In 1993, a referendum for autonomy was organized in Narva (and in the nearby town of Sillamäe), potentially as a prelude to secession. While a majority of people in Narva voted for independence, the town's government decided to respect the opinion of an Estonian court, which ruled the vote illegal.[45] There are concerns that Russia could engineer another separatist movement in Narva or another border Russian-dominated town (Daugavpils in Latvia's Latgale region is also often identified as potentially vulnerable to Russian subversion).[46]

Under current conditions, Narva and other Russian-majority towns in Estonia or Latvia are not particularly fertile ground for a separatist movement. Pro-Russian organizations in Estonia and Latvia have pursued greater language rights and have adopted the anti-fascist rhetoric put out by Moscow, but none appears to have pursued a separatist agenda.[47] In interviews with journalists, residents of Narva and other towns in the region consistently downplay any desire to rebel against Estonia or join Russia, and these accounts often highlight how the experience of the residents traveling across the river to Ivangorod in Russia further discourages them from

---

[44] Douglas Mastriano, "Defeating Putin's Strategy of Ambiguity," *War on the Rocks*, November 6, 2014.

[45] Lisa Trei, "Estonian Towns Vote for Autonomy," *The Moscow Times*, July 20, 1993.

[46] A *New York Times* article notes,

> In a recent article urging Russia to undertake a "preventive occupation" of this and two other Baltic nations, all of them NATO members, Rostislav Ishchenko, a political analyst close to influential nationalist figures in Moscow, asserted that Latgale's separate identity could help open the way for a "revision" of Baltic borders. A map accompanying the article showed Latgale as a separate entity taking up the entire length of what is now Latvia's border with Russia. . . . Latvia's Security Police, the domestic intelligence agency, have struggled to trace the source of the appeals but believe they originated in Russia. "They seem to be some kind of provocation to test how we would react," said a security agency official, who asked not to be identified because of the delicacy of the issue. He said there were no signs of separatist fervor in Latgale itself and described the Latgalian People's Republic as an "artificial creation by outsiders." (Andrew Higgins, "Latvian Region Has Distinct Identity, and Allure for Russia," *New York Times*, May 20, 2015)

[47] Discussions with Estonian and Latvian officials and analysts, Tallinn and Riga, July 2015. Note also that Estonian and Latvian security services do not specifically observe groups voicing separatism. Estonia Internal Security Service, 2013, pp. 5–9; Latvia Security Police, 2013, pp. 10–12.

pursuing separatism.[48] Katri Raik, the director of Narva College in Estonia, similarly notes, "What would happen if Narva were to hold a referendum? Would its residents want to live in Estonia or in Putin's Russia? Anyone with any common sense . . . would want to live in Estonia."[49] Even the former leader of the 1993 Narva autonomy referendum appears relatively content with the political status quo.[50] During my visit to Narva in July 2015, there seemed little evidence of tension that might escalate to violence.[51]

Of course, a strong desire for separatism was not evident in eastern Ukraine prior to 2014, so the insistence of residents is not necessarily evidence that a similar situation could not arise in the Baltics. Even without the use of violence, Russia could covertly infiltrate pro-Russian groups in Estonia or Latvia to influence their policies and preferences, or organize relatively few individuals into a new movement. But there are significant demographic and social differences between the Russian-dominated areas of the Baltic states and eastern Ukraine that would likely prevent a significant portion of the population from joining a separatist movement. Unlike Russian areas of Estonia and Latvia, eastern Ukraine was closely integrated into Russia politically and economically for many years. Russian speakers in the Baltic countries are generally relatively better off than many in Russia and are unlikely to be motivated by the same

---

[48] Interviews with Estonian and Latvia academics and staff of think tanks, Riga and Tallinn, July 2015. One article gave the example of Alexandr Brokk, a Russian-speaking resident of Narva, who feels affinity toward Russia, but remains an "Estonian patriot":

> "People come and go. When you cross into Ivangorod, straight away you can see the atmosphere there," Brokk says. "Who is going to want to join that?" Brokk's opinions are not an anomaly here. In Narva, Russian is the lingua franca, Russian media is the main source of news, and orange-and-black St. George ribbons symbolizing military victory adorn cars. But the Russians of Narva . . . call the European Union and NATO their home. And while they may feel the emotional tug of Moscow and certainly have their grievances with the Estonian government in Tallinn, few say they want to follow the example of Crimea and join Russia. (Tom Balmforth, "Russians of Narva Not Seeking 'Liberation' by Moscow," Radio Free Europe/Radio Liberty, April 4, 2014)

[49] Raik further notes, "People in Narva know what they would choose because they often travel to Ivangorod [in Russia]" (quoted in Robert Person, "6 Reasons Not to Worry about Russia Invading the Baltics," *Washington Post,* November 12, 2015).

[50] A *Wall Street Journal* article in July 2014 described the leader of the referendum:

> I caught up with [Mr. Chuikin] in Tallinn. Over the past two decades, he had gone into business and retired. Now in his early 60s, he still hasn't learned Estonian or obtained citizenship. He shows off his Russian passport, even though he has lived most of his life in Estonia. He's monolingual and gripes that the young Estonian hostess at the coffee shop where we meet doesn't speak Russian. Mr. Chuikin recently moved to a new suburban home in Tallinn next door to his daughter, who married an ethnic Estonian and has bilingual children. His other daughter moved to Stockholm, married a Swede and is raising her own multilingual kids. Every few weeks, he makes the quick flight over the Baltic Sea to see them. His Estonian residency permit lets him travel around Europe without a visa. He enjoys a European life and admires Vladimir Putin. (Matthew Kaminski, "The Town Where the Russian Dilemma Lives," *Wall Street Journal,* July 4, 2014)

[51] There was certainly evidence of Russian nationalism, including a Russian flag on an all-terrain vehicle participating in a motorcycle rally.

economic factors that appear to have facilitated separatism in eastern Ukraine.[52] None of this implies that it would be impossible for Russia to organize a protest or separatist movement, but rather that such a movement would probably not have the local support necessary to camouflage its origins from Estonian, Latvian, or even NATO authorities. The absence of local support would undermine the ambiguity of Russian subversion and make it more likely that there would be a strong NATO and EU response.

Russia clearly has an incentive to use nonviolent means to radicalize Russian speakers living in the Baltics to gain influence in the region. Russia may hope to encourage a separatist movement that would undermine the sovereignty of the Baltic countries and thereby guarantees of the EU and NATO, or may hope to use its influence to encourage the Baltic countries to adopt policies more friendly to Russian influence. While the Russian minorities in Estonia and Latvia do give Russia a variety of options and points of influence for subversion, the actual ability of Russian agents to mobilize the Russian minority in the Baltics appears quite limited, especially given the high level of integration of many in the Baltics and their relatively high standard of living relative to that of Russians on the other side of the border.

## Covert Violent Action

A second general category of hybrid Russian aggression, not necessarily mutually exclusive with nonviolent subversion, is the use of covert or denied violence by Russian forces. Russian covert action might seek to undermine the Western agenda of Euro-Atlantic integration by indicating that the West would not or could not protect the sovereignty of the Baltic countries.

Western analysts often highlight a scenario drawn from Russian activities in Crimea, in which significant numbers of unmarked Russia Spetsnaz seize control of a town or city dominated by Russian speakers, such as Narva in Estonia or Daugavpils in Latvia.[53] A local pro-Russian political movement could declare independence, invite Russian forces into the territory to support their objectives, and encourage Russia to annex the territory. Covert action might make it difficult for NATO or its member states to attribute the secession to Russian aggression, which could undermine a NATO response. Russian annexation might also deter NATO from responding by indicating that Russia would go to war with NATO or use nuclear weapons to defend its territory. Russia's conventional forces might play a role in deterring a response by the Baltic countries or other NATO members, but would not cross over the border. Indeed, limiting the presence of Russia's conventional forces on the territory of the Baltic countries could be essential to reducing the likelihood of a strong response by NATO.

---

[52] Zhukov, 2014.

[53] For details on the Russian Spetsnaz activities in Crimea, see Charles Bartles and Roger McDermott, "Russia's Military Operation in Crimea," *Problems of Post-Communism*, Vol. 61, No. 6, 2014, pp. 57–58. These scenarios draw from discussions with U.S. and NATO officials and analysts, June and July 2015, and February 2016.

In a second covert scenario, following the model of Russian activities in eastern Ukraine in mid-2014, Russian could offer limited covert support and encouragement for a separatist movement. Russian intelligence or special operations forces could co-opt and encourage local pro-Russian movements to declare a separatist agenda. Russia might provide arms and advice rather than significant numbers of forces. Rather than attempting to control territory, in this scenario Russian-backed groups could operate covertly, attacking the government forces. Russia would be creating instability within an EU and NATO member, thereby undermining the alliance's credibility. As with the first scenario, Russia's ability to act covertly could be essential to prevent NATO from attributing the political conflict to Russian involvement.

A third scenario, raised by a former Latvian official, is the possibility of Russia instigating a terrorist campaign against the Baltic governments. Russian agents could, for example, attack Russian speakers visiting a Soviet monument, pretending that it was the work of Baltic fascists. Russian agents then could facilitate the development of terrorist cells to undertake attacks within the Baltic capitals.[54]

In each of these scenarios, especially the second and third, Russia could deny its presence and claim that any action was carried out by the local population. As one analyst in the Baltics explained, such forces are more likely to be appear as "men in jeans" rather than "little green men" in uniforms without insignia, making more plausible Russia's claim that no Russian forces are involved in any violence.[55] The success of Russia's efforts depends on two factors: (1) the ability of the Baltic countries to clearly attribute Russian aggression and gain support from its fellow NATO members and (2) the ability of the separatist/Russian forces to hold off the Baltic security forces. The ability of the Baltic countries to control their territory and to limit the movement and freedom of action of covert Russian forces will undermine Russian objectives in the first scenario and make insurgent/separatist activities under the second and third scenarios far more difficult.

Like Crimea and eastern Ukraine, the eastern portions of Estonia and Latvia are proximate to Russia and do have a significant Russian-speaking population that might make them similarly vulnerable to Russian covert action. In general, however, the Baltic countries appear to be a less fertile ground for covert subversion than Ukraine. While Russia was able to seize and maintain control over Crimea, where its conventional forces maintained dominance, the success of covert actions in eastern Ukraine was ultimately less successful, as discussed above. The Baltic countries are better positioned than Ukraine to defend against and deter Russian covert action. They have greater control over their own territory, through the development of their internal security forces, as outlined below. Furthermore, they are members of NATO, and so benefit from

---

[54] There are of course other scenarios for Russian covert action, although the effectiveness of each them centers around the ability of Baltic forces to identify, attribute, and stop Russian activities. Interview with former Latvian official, Riga, July 2015.

[55] Interview with think tank analyst, Riga, July 2015.

assistance from other NATO countries, including under Article 5. Unlike Ukraine, where NATO support to Ukraine was limited to nonlethal equipment after Russia used conventional forces to support the separatists, NATO member countries are committed to respond to an attack on any of the Baltic states as if it were an attack on themselves.

Indeed, both Estonian and Latvian Ministry of Defence officials indicated confidence in their ability to deal with covert Russian activity because of their greater state capacity and NATO's conventional deterrent.[56] Their policy to address covert Russian aggression is relatively straightforward—they plan to shoot the "little green men."[57] The Estonian Chief of Defence explains, "If Russian agents or special forces enter Estonian territory, 'you should shoot the first one to appear. . . . If somebody without any military insignia commits terrorist attacks in your country you should shoot him . . . you should not allow them to enter."[58] By rapidly deploying civilian and military forces to quickly defeat Russian covert elements, the Baltic countries hope to defeat Russian special forces, and leave Russia with the choice of either backing down or risking conventional escalation that would bring NATO into the war. By relying on NATO to provide a conventional deterrent, the Baltic states thereby hope to deter Russian covert action.[59]

This strategy is uncertain, however. In practice, the Baltic countries may hesitate before attacking Russian forces operating in their territory because of fears of Russia's willingness to escalate. Russia may also be able to seize territory and establish a new status quo before the Baltic states are able to respond. Indeed, the Baltic countries recognize the importance of rapidly alerting NATO of Russian aggression under Article 4 or 5.[60] The Baltic countries may also not

---

[56] One Latvian defense official, for example, noted that their concern was not little green men or a limited conventional attack, but a large-scale conventional invasion. Estonian officials offered a similar perspective. Interviews with Latvian and Estonian defense officials, Riga and Tallinn, July 2015.

[57] The *New York Times* reported, "Asked what steps his military would take if Russian 'little green men' tried to sneak across his border, General Riho Terras, Estonia's chief of defense, said bluntly, 'We will shoot them'" (Eric Schmitt and Steve Lee Myers, "NATO Refocuses on the Kremlin, Its Original Foe," *New York Times*, June 23, 2015). See also Andrew Stuttaford, "On Shooting 'Little Green Men,'" *National Review*, May 14, 2015. Similar remarks were apparently made by Raimonds Vējonis, the former defense minister and current president in Latvia (interviews with Latvian defense officials, Riga, July 2015).

[58] General Terras, the Estonian chief of defense, explains in the *Financial Times*,

> "Hybrid warfare is nothing new. You can deal with it only with the cohesion of the nation, with integrity, with all society working together . . . [Estonia] is a functioning society," he stressed. "We are not like Ukraine. . . . But we need to be very well aware of what is happening in Russia and be ready." Most importantly, Gen Terras said, NATO needed to be prepared to stand behind his country and go to war in the event of his forces having to forcibly confront any Russian interference in a way that Kiev was initially unable to do. (Sam Jones, "Estonia Ready to Deal with Little Green Men," *Financial Times*, May 13, 2015)

[59] Interviews and discussions with Estonian and Latvian officials, Tallinn, Riga, and Washington, D.C., July 2015 and November 2015.

[60] Article 4 simply states that the parties will consult whenever "in the opinion of any of them, the territorial integrity, political independence or security of any of the Parties is threatened." Article 5 says that "The Parties agree that an armed attack against one or more of them in Europe or North America shall be considered an attack against them all," and states that the members will take "such action as it deems necessary, including the use of

receive full NATO support if the presence of Russian forces is ambiguous and there is reason to believe that opposition is primarily carried out by Baltic Russian speakers.

Hence, despite the confidence of the Baltic officials, it remains important to evaluate the readiness, capabilities, and coordination of the security forces in the Baltic countries. Estonia appears have a relatively well-prepared security structure, albeit small and dependent on rapid mobilization of reservists. Estonia has an active duty ground force of 5,500 soldiers, of whom 2,700 are conscripts, organized into two brigades. With the exception of one professional high-readiness mechanized battalion, these two brigades are at low readiness and mainly serve to train conscripts for eight to 11 months before they are moved into the reserves.[61] There are also four teams of American-trained special operations forces, who have repeatedly deployed to Afghanistan. The Kaitseliit, a 15,000-strong National Guard, contains some well-trained and -equipped fighting units that would coordinate with the special operations forces in the event of an invasion. Based on their own estimates of Russian special forces capabilities, Estonian officials claim that a two-battalion force—their own plus a U.S. or NATO battalion—would be able to hold off Russian special forces, at least until a broader mobilization occurred.[62]

Estonian government officials are confident in their ability to monitor Russian activity within their territory, highlighting the capability of the Internal Security Service, although it is uncertain how effectively this information can be shared with other NATO members. A July 2015 visit to Narva revealed a modern multilayered border post that would require a not insignificant effort to circumvent.[63] While Western officials were skeptical of the extent of coordination between the Ministry of Defence and internal security forces, Estonian government officials claimed that coordination was quite good and straightforward in large part due to the small size of the Estonian security establishment. Estonia has undertaken regular war games and exercises to understand how to respond to different forms of Russian aggression, including practicing handoffs of responsibilities from the internal security forces to the Ministry of Defence forces and determining when to seek assistance from NATO. The Hedgehog exercise in May 2015, for

---

armed force, to restore and maintain the security of the North Atlantic area" (NATO, "The North Atlantic Treaty," April 4, 1949).

[61] Jane's World Armies, "Estonia," 2015.

[62] Jane's World Armies, "Estonia," 2015; interviews with Estonian officials, July 2015.

[63] However, there was a recent case of an Estonian border guard being captured and imprisoned by Russia, perhaps questioning the ability of Estonian border guards to defend themselves. Estonian officials attribute the kidnapping due to the investigation by the border agent of smuggling in the region by Russian government forces. Russia sentenced the official to 15 years in prison on espionage charges in August 2015. See BBC, "Russia Jails Estonia Security Official Eston Kohver," August 19, 2015b; Corey Flintoff, "Estonia 'Spy' Dispute Could Be Russia Making Anti-NATO Mischief," NPR, September 14, 2014.

example, involved 13,000 Estonian personnel and revealed gaps in mobilization times that the government is currently seeking to address.[64]

The readiness and preparation of the Latvian military is more questionable. Despite Latvia's greater population (2 million compared with 1.3 million in Estonia), Latvian forces are smaller than Estonia's, in large part because Latvia spends only 0.94 percent of GDP on defense, in comparison with Estonia's 1.93 percent in 2014.[65] Latvia does not have conscription, and the overall size of the active ground force is 3,900. This force is organized into a single brigade with two active duty battalions, and also includes highly trained special forces. Latvia also has a volunteer National Guard of approximately 8,000.[66] The focus of the military has been on out-of-area NATO deployments, and some Western trained observers in Riga have expressed doubts about the force's readiness to counter either serious covert violent action or a conventional attack.[67] As with Estonia, Latvian officials were also confident of their intelligence gathering related to Russian covert actions. They observed that they had dealt with the Russian covert threat for many years. Although Latvian defense officials noted good interagency information sharing, contingency planning, and coordination,[68] Western-trained observers noted serious interagency coordination problems, including the absence of regular exercises to practice crisis coordination between the Ministry of Defence and internal security forces. Latvian and foreign observers have also questioned the effectiveness of the Latvian border guard relative to those of Estonia and the Nordic countries.[69]

Additional research is necessary to fully evaluate the tactical ability of the Baltic forces to respond to Russian covert action. Further investigation of Russian tactics in Ukraine and other contingencies and of Russian capabilities for engaging in covert activities even in the presence of opposing security forces would be useful. A more detailed investigation of the Baltic countries' forces could also help illuminate gaps in areas such as training, equipment, and doctrine. Nevertheless, the Baltic countries are high-functioning European states that have control throughout their territory. Officials in Estonia and, to a lesser extent, Latvia have practiced their response to Russian action, and there is good reason to believe that they would be able to deploy sufficient forces to respond to the presence of limited numbers of Russian covert forces.

---

[64] Interview with Estonian defense and Western officials, Tallinn, July 2015. Ben Farmer and David Blair, "Estonia Stages Biggest Military Exercise in Country's History Amid Fears of Russian 'Aggression,'" *The Telegraph*, May 12, 2015.

[65] NATO, "Defence Expenditures of NATO Countries (2008–2015)," January 28, 2016.

[66] Jane's World's Armies, "Latvia," 2015.

[67] Interview with former Western officer, Riga, July 2015.

[68] Interviews with Latvian defense officials, Riga, July 2015.

[69] Discussions with former Latvian official, former Western officer, and Western advisors, Riga, March and July 2015. See Robert Nurick and Magnus Nordenman, eds., "Nordic-Baltic Security in the 21st Century: The Regional Agenda and the Global Role," *The Atlantic Council*, September 2011, p. 3.

## Conventional Aggression Supported by Political Subversion

A final category of hybrid warfare involves a conventional attack by Russian ground, air, naval, and airborne forces, justified and legitimized by covert or denied activities focused on the Russian speakers. Such an attack could seek to capture territory, replace the government of the Baltic countries, or shift the military balance in an ongoing internal conflict, as in eastern Ukraine. Even if the value to Russia of occupying the Baltic countries is low, Russia could seek to demonstrate that NATO's security guarantees are not credible and the United States is unable to defend its allies.

Russian conventional forces could adopt a range of courses of action. They might seek to drive ground forces across the Baltic countries to their capitals, and attempt to seize the countries before a significant Western response. Russian forces might limit their offensive to a small "bite" of the Baltic countries, capturing a Russian-dominated city near the border, such as Narva, or an area of strategic importance, such as a land bridge between Belarus and Kaliningrad. Russia may bargain that NATO is unwilling to risk war to recapture an area of strategic importance to Russia, or a Russian-dominated territory where there is some ambiguity about whether there is support for Russian action by the local population. Russia would likely use its anti-access and area-denial capabilities to inhibit NATO deployments in the region and give it more time to consolidate its gains. However Russia uses its conventional forces, it will likely threaten the use of nuclear weapons to deter a response from NATO. Russia has discussed the possibility of deploying tactical nuclear weapons to Crimea and nuclear-capable ballistic Iskander missiles to Kaliningrad, and emphasized that it would use such weapons to defend its territory. Russia would likely do the same if it attacked the Baltics.[70]

RAND has recently undertaken a series of tabletop exercises to better understand the prospects for a Russian conventional attack in the Baltics. Based on open source estimates, Russia could muster approximately 27 maneuver battalion tactical groups to attack the Baltic countries in a short-warning attack, supported by significant long-range fires. Assuming a week of warning, NATO could deploy 12 maneuver battalions. NATO forces, however, would be light, outgunned, and outmaneuvered by Russian heavier units, and fixed in place or destroyed while Russian forces maneuvered toward the capitals. Furthermore, while NATO could deploy significant air forces, without heavy NATO ground forces present, Russia would have significant freedom to deploy its forces to limit its vulnerability to air power. Across multiple iterations of the scenario, Russian forces were on the outskirts of Riga and Tallinn between 36 and 60 hours after the start of the war. It would likely take at least several weeks until armored reinforcements from the United States could arrive in numbers that would be capable of ejecting Russian forces.

---

[70] Zachery Keck, "Russia Threatens to Deploy Nuclear Weapons in Crimea," *National Interest*, June 1, 2015; Laura Smith-Spark, Alla Eshchenko and Emma Burrows, "Russia Was Ready to Put Nuclear Forces on Alert over Crimea, Putin Says," *CNN*, March 16, 2015; Matthew Bodner, "Kremlin Threatens Response to U.S. Nuclear Bomb Deployment in Germany," *The Moscow Times*, September 23, 2015.

By that point, NATO may be reluctant to risk nuclear war and bear the heavy casualties necessary to retake the Russian-occupied areas in the Baltics.[71] The success of Russia's actions in the "small bite" scenario may vary depending on the degree of surprise, but the chances for Russia's conventional success in the short term appear high, given the substantial numerical superiority of Russian conventional forces in the region.

While Russia could theoretically only use conventional forces and eschew political subversion or covert action, these unconventional tactics have the potential to reduce the likelihood of a NATO response. Russia could provoke a conflict between Russian speakers and the Baltic governments, which may create the perception that local Russian speakers support Russian military action. Because the North Atlantic Council makes decisions based on consensus, any disagreement about Russian intent could delay or vitiate a NATO-backed response to Russian provocations. Russian leaders made an extensive effort to rationalize and justify their actions in Crimea, and it seems likely that Russian aggression in the future would be accompanied by similar activities to justify their actions.[72] Russian covert action could also be used to delay or undermine the Baltic countries' ability to deploy their security forces to respond to Russian forces.

Even in the absence of consensus within the North Atlantic Council, individual member states could come to the defense of the Baltics under Article 5, which states that each member state can take "such action at it deems necessary, including the use of armed force, to restore and maintain the security of the North Atlantic area."[73] So long as the United States is willing to respond, and the transit countries of Germany and Poland permit the U.S. deployment, opposition from other member states cannot prevent a large-scale military response to a potential Russian invasion.

In summary, the greatest danger posed by Russia in the Baltics appears to be its local conventional superiority. Without the threat or actual use of a conventional attack to inhibit a decisive response to Russian subversion, the efficacy of nonviolent or covert efforts would be limited against competent states such as the Baltics. Offsetting Russia's geographic advantages with a strengthened NATO defense posture may therefore be the essential precondition for maintaining political stability in this region. The nature of such a deterrent is the focus on other research and beyond the scope of this report.[74] It suffices to note that such a deterrent will likely involve a significant deployment of NATO forces to the region. The Baltic countries, for example, have requested that the United States permanently deploy a U.S. Army battalion in each country. Determining the types and numbers of forces and where they will be deployed will

---

[71] See David A. Shlapak and Michael Johnson, *Reinforcing Deterrence on NATO's Eastern Flank: Wargaming the Defense of the Baltics*, Santa Monica, Calif.: RAND Corporation, RR-1253-A, 2015, pp. 1–8.

[72] Allison, 2014.

[73] NATO, 1949.

[74] See, for example, Shlapak and Johnson, 2015.

have important ramifications for the relations between the Russian speakers and their governments.

# 4. Policy Implications

This report concludes that the major vulnerability to hybrid warfare in the Baltics lies in Russian conventional forces that may "back up" or accompany nonviolent or covert Russian aggression. This does not mean that the United States and NATO can focus solely on providing an effective conventional deterrent and ignore other threats. Rather, it will be important that NATO strengthen its defense and deterrence at all levels of conflict, ranging from propaganda and cyber warfare, to covert action, to conventional warfare. By reducing the vulnerabilities of the Baltics, and reducing Russian perceptions that it can exploit the vulnerabilities of the Baltic states, the potential for conflict and escalation is diminished. Actions to address these vulnerabilities may also be beneficial for other reasons. For example, better integration of Russian speakers may help to build more-cohesive societies in the Baltics. It is also important to consider the risk that NATO's efforts to strengthen deterrence of a conventional attack may increase the vulnerability to nonviolent or covert Russian action. Prodded by Russian propaganda and absent effective NATO messaging, Russian speakers in the Baltics may interpret NATO's actions as intended to encircle or threaten Russia, or to exercise control over the Baltic countries, and may thereby become more likely to engage in opposition.

## Integration of Russians

The first set of possible policy responses concern how to advance the integration of Russian speakers within each of the Baltic countries. There are two basic ways to address this issue. The first is to increase political and civic rights for Russian speakers, especially with regard to citizenship, education, and official recognition of the Russian language. Greater recognition of the Russian language, increased funding for Russian-language education, and citizenship for Soviet-era migrants would diminish Moscow's influence by undermining the idea that the Baltic states do not welcome Russian speakers. The EU did put significant pressure on Estonia and Latvia to grant greater rights to the Russian minority during and following accession negotiations, and there are reports of ongoing discussions about increasing rights for the Russian minority.[1] The problem, however, is that granting greater rights to Russian speakers is to some extent in conflict with the nationalist narratives surrounding the creation of Estonia and Latvia. The Baltic countries have made significant progress in integrating the Russian-speaking population and recognizing the legitimate role of Russian speakers who learn the titular language and are loyal to their country. Nevertheless, there remains a widespread view that further compromise to the Russian-speaking population, who represent a legacy of occupation, would

---

[1] Julia Ioffe, "Ethnic Russians in the Baltics Are Actually Persecuted. So Why Isn't Putin Stepping In?" *New Republic*, March 11, 2014; Kasekamp, 2010, pp. 184–191.

undermine the survival of their countries as independent states.[2] Estonian and Latvian leaders' rejection of the likelihood of Russian subversion may in part be motivated by a desire to avoid consideration of additional compromises in the direction of rights for Russian speakers. While the European Union, or EU member states such as Germany, do have a great deal of influence among the Baltic states, the practical influence of these countries over the domestic policy of the Baltic countries is limited—citizenship, education, and related issues are clearly the prerogative of the Baltic countries themselves. The importance and sensitivity of the position of the Russian-speaking population in Estonia and Latvia means that even private pressure from Western countries is liable to be a waste of effort or even counterproductive.

A second area where Western attention could have a greater impact is in the field of strategic communications. There has been much discussion of efforts to counter Russian propaganda. The EU considered creating a pan-European Russian-language station but has instead settled on developing content for local media stations in Eastern Neighborhood countries such as Georgia and Ukraine.[3] Estonia has established the Russian-language television station ETV+, which will broadcast in Russian, while Latvia's parallel effort to establish a Russian-language TV station confronted political and economic difficulties.[4] Continued funding for Russian-language broadcasts by Deutsch Welle, Radio Free Europe/Radio Liberty, or other Western government–funded networks could help around the margins, but content directly funded by Western countries is unlikely to be credible.[5] Steve Tatham, for example, criticizes Western official information campaigns and urges greater social science research to understand the Baltic populations and thereby better direct NATO's strategic communications efforts.[6] Indeed, further

---

[2] Francesco Duina and Carlo Miani, "Fitting in the Baltics: National Identity, Minorities and Compliance with EU Accession Requirements in Lithuania and Latvia," *Comparative European Politics*, Vol. 13, No. 5, September 2015, pp. 535–552.

[3] Interview with European External Action Service official, Brussels, June 17, 2015; Rikard Jozwiak, "EU Plans to Step Up Fight Against Russian Propaganda," Radio Free Europe/Radio Liberty, June 24, 2015.

[4] One Latvian think tank analyst explained that the effort to develop a state-funded Russian-language program was blocked because it was problematic for the Latvian government to fund broadcasts not in the official language of Latvian. Interview with think tank analyst, Riga, July 2015; "TV in Russian: Estonia Leads the Way," *The Baltic Review*, August 20, 2015; Matthew Luxmoore, "Latvia Struggles with Restive Russian Minority Amid Regional Tensions," *Al Jazeera America*, June 13, 2015.

[5] Anton Troianovski, "Germany Seeks to Counter Russian 'Propaganda' in Baltics," *Wall Street Journal*, April 17, 2015.

[6] He writes,

> Our collective messaging tends . . . to be led not by an innate understanding of audiences but by creativity and follows the ideas of policy makers in Brussels, London and Washington. The principle is "This is the message—send it out"; invariably that message is crafted by European or North American men in suits sat behind a computer in an office. . . . Both Hitler and Putin are (were) very good at propaganda. NATO and the EU are not but nor do they need to be so; the answer to propaganda is not more propaganda. The answer is to properly understand its effect and put in the place the necessary mitigation—which may not be communication—to extinguish its flames. (Steve Tatham, "The Solution to Russian Propaganda Is Not EU or NATO Propaganda but

in-depth survey and focus group research will be valuable in understanding the socioeconomic and political concerns of the Russian speakers, and help enable Western engagement and strategic communication to better respond to their concerns, beliefs, and perceptions. In the short term, additional funding for the Estonian and Latvian government-supported Russian-language television stations may be the best available option. The relatively small audience makes it difficult to develop a functioning station with reasonable production values. A modicum of Western funding and support could help create stations that provide a relevant, objective, and competitive alternative to the Moscow-controlled stations.

## Countering Covert Action

Improving the response to potential Russian covert action can be thought of in three phases: detecting and attributing Russian action, strengthening the capacity of the Baltics to respond, and formulating an effective and appropriate EU and NATO response.

Better intelligence gathering and coordination and a clearer understanding of the signs of Russian covert aggression can help bolster defenses against active subversion. U.S. Air Force assets, such as unmanned aerial vehicles and ground-based radars, could be beneficial at filling gaps in these countries' existing intelligence, surveillance, and reconnaissance capabilities, both for covert action and conventional warfare.[7] NATO is also currently undertaking several initiatives to improve intelligence and coordination related to Russian covert action, including developing shared indicators and warnings, NATO Force Integration Units (NFIUs), and combined exercises. Although NATO has made progress in developing institutions for intelligence sharing, NATO's structures and processes for intelligence sharing remain cumbersome and dependent on often-reluctant nations to share.[8] Given NATO's slow progress in this area, further developing bilateral intelligence sharing between the Baltic countries and the United States or other NATO countries could be valuable. Additional research could also contribute by identifying the signs and mechanisms of past instances of large-scale Russian covert activities in Georgia, Crimea, and eastern Ukraine. So far, there is little open source information about how to differentiate between "everyday" Russian exercises and influence operations and the start of a large-scale campaign mirroring the operation in Crimea. More

Advanced Social Science to Understand and Mitigate Its Effect in Targeted Populations," *National Defense Academy of Latvia*, Policy Paper No. 4, July 2015, pp. 4, 9)

[7] Recent RAND research considers the opportunities for engagement in the Baltics in more detail—see Christopher S. Chivvis, Raphael S. Cohen, Bryan Frederick, Daniel S. Hamilton, F. Stephen Larrabee, and Bonny Lin, *NATO's Northeastern Flank: Emerging Opportunities for Engagement*, Santa Monica, Calif.: RAND Corporation, RR-1467-AF, forthcoming.

[8] Brian R. Foster, *Enhancing the Efficiency of NATO Intelligence Under an ASG-I*, Carlisle Barracks, Pa.: U.S. Army War College, Strategy Research Project, 2013; "US Commander Says NATO Will Bolster Intelligence-Sharing Among Military Alliance's Members," Associated Press, April 30, 2015.

clearly identifying the *modus operandi* of Russian agents would help to separate out the cases that justify a NATO deployment and those that might not.

The capacity of the Baltic countries to counter covert action can certainly be improved. U.S. special operations forces have conducted extensive engagement with their Baltic counterparts, to the point that there is a sense of saturation, especially given the small size of the Baltic special operations forces. Additional research may be beneficial to help identify gaps in the Baltic countries' capacity, including within civilian agencies, and to conduct targeted missions that could offer more focused benefits. Support for the Baltic states to counter covert action may also strengthen their ability to resist Russia in the event of an invasion.[9] The U.S. Air Force may be able to directly assist with the development of technical capabilities for border control, air and maritime domain awareness, and intelligence gathering, including assistance with acquiring unmanned aerial vehicles, radars, and other sensors. Another specific area where the United States may be able to offer assistance is in planning exercises and war games to improve contingency planning and coordination, especially in Latvia.

Finally, the United States, NATO, and the Baltic countries can do more to think practically through how a response to Russian covert action would proceed. The 2014 Wales Summit focused on the development of greater "responsiveness" through the Readiness Action Plan and the creation of the Very High Readiness Joint Task Force (VJTF). However, it remains uncertain how these new, more responsive forces would be employed if there was warning of a significant Russian covert (or conventional) military action in the Baltics.[10] While the development of the VJTF and implementation of the Readiness Action Plan is complex and will take time, it is highly beneficial for the United States and other NATO allies to think through on a practical level how a high-readiness forces would deploy and be employed in the Baltics, and how they would coordinate its actions with the Baltic security forces.

## Avoiding the Risk of Conventional Deterrence Initiatives Fomenting Irregular Provocation

Russian propaganda harps on the theme of NATO's aggressive intentions, and any buildup of NATO forces will inevitably feed into Russia depictions of NATO as seeking to encircle and isolate Russia.[11] In a March 2015 poll in Estonia, for example, 64 percent of Russian speakers stated that they were either "rather against" or "certainly against" a NATO deployment in

---

[9] See Jan Osburg, *Unconventional Options for the Defense of the Baltic States: The Swiss Approach*, Santa Monica, Calif.: RAND Corporation, PE-179-RC, 2016.

[10] Discussions with U.S. and NATO officials, Brussels, Mons, and Washington, D.C., June and August 2015. See also NATO, "Wales Summit Declaration," September 5, 2014.

[11] See "NATO Destabilizing Baltic by Stationing Nuke-Capable Aircraft—Moscow," *Russia Today*, December 1, 2014; "'Unprecedented and Dangerous Step': Russia Slams NATO Troop Build-Up," *Russia Today*, April 2, 2015.

Estonia, compared with only 8 percent of Estonian speakers.[12] There is a reasonable concern that the presence of significant U.S. or NATO forces could further shift the opinions of Russian speakers toward Moscow and make the population more susceptible to Russian influence. While the deployment of NATO conventional forces to the region may make conventional war less likely, it may paradoxically increase the risk of Russian subversion and lower-intensity conflict, with the associated potential for escalation. Based on the findings above, nonviolent subversion and covert action will likely remain difficult, but the risk of Russian action, miscalculation, and/or escalation could increase. Although U.S. Army deployments in the Baltics may be larger in numbers of personnel, the same challenges of avoiding provoking opposition from local Russian speakers apply to U.S. Air Force deployments, such as the recent deployment of A-10s.[13]

This is not to argue that the deployment of U.S. or NATO forces is ill-advised, but rather that it is important to manage perceptions of these initiatives, in part by considering carefully where, how, and which forces are deployed. There is no way to prevent Russian propaganda from misrepresenting U.S. or NATO activities in the Baltics, or from claiming that U.S. or NATO actions are provocative. The United States and NATO can, however, take pains to reduce the risk that a deployment will increase the vulnerability to irregular Russian aggression, or that Russia will take preventative action because it misperceives a U.S. or NATO deployment as threatening its security.

First, NATO should avoid basing forces in heavily Russian-speaking areas. Whatever the reality, NATO forces could be perceived as occupying forces, and any accidents or confrontations between Russian-speaking civilians and NATO personnel have the potential to escalate. To some extent, this limitation poses a challenge for a response to a covert or limited conventional Russian action against a Russian-dominated border area. NATO forces far away from the border might have difficulty reacting quickly, and Russia may be able to seize a small amount of territory as a *fait accompli*. Nevertheless, the need to avoid possible provocation might justify the added risk. To date, NATO forces do not appear to have been based in Russian-dominated areas. Thus far in Estonia, for example, rotational forces are mainly based at Tapa and the Amari airfield.[14]

Second, while Russia will inevitably exaggerate the intention of NATO to use its position in the Baltics to undermine the regime, the Russian leadership is clearly concerned about the potential for NATO forces in the region being used to support a color revolution or other action to depose the regime.[15] Even if such claims are not justified, Russian leaders may be motivated

---

[12] Juhan Kivirähk, "Public Opinion and National Defence," Estonian Ministry of Defence, April 2015, p. 50.

[13] See, for example, the recent deployment of A-10s beginning in September 2015, Jennifer Svan, "US A-10s Arrive in Estonia for 6 Month Rotation," *Stars and Stripes,* September 22, 2015.

[14] Interview with Estonian Ministry of Defence officials, Tallinn, July 16, 2015.

[15] Gorenburg, 2015.

to take preventative action against U.S. or NATO forces if they believe that these forces pose an imminent threat to the regime. The United States and NATO cannot prevent misperception, but they can take action to improve transparency or limit activities or forces that might be perceived to be intended for regime change, such as operations in support of the Russian opposition or weapon systems that could be used to disable Russia's command and control networks.

Finally, the development of a sound public relations campaign associated with U.S. forces in the Baltics is critical. The provision of services by U.S. or NATO civil affairs teams is highly beneficial, especially in predominately Russian-speaking areas. For example, there are reports of U.S. soldiers helping to rebuild an orphanage and pursuing other humanitarian missions.[16] While such activities may appear heavy-handed, if managed carefully and if coordinated with the local government, they can help convince local Russians that NATO is not deploying forces against them.

---

[16] Interviews with U.S. and Latvian officials, Riga, July 15, 2015; see also 7th Mobile Public Affairs Detachment, "Sky Soldiers Give Back," July 12, 2015.

# References

7th Mobile Public Affairs Detachment, "Sky Soldiers Give Back," July 12, 2015. As of June 20, 2016:
https://www.dvidshub.net/video/414894/sky-soldiers-give-back#.Vc3fxr4zyfQ

Adamsky, Dmitry (Dima), "Cross-Domain Coercion: The Current Russian Art of Strategy," Institut Français des Relations Internationales, November 2015. As of June 20, 2016:
http://www.ifri.org/sites/default/files/atoms/files/pp54adamsky.pdf

"Address of President of Ukraine Petro Poroshenko," July 1, 2014. As of June 20, 2016:
http://www.president.gov.ua/en/news/zvernennya-prezidenta-ukrayini-petra-poroshenka-33119

Allison, Roy, "Russian 'Deniable' Intervention in Ukraine: How and Why Russia Broke the Rules," *International Affairs*, Vol. 90, No. 6, 2014, pp. 1255–1268.

Balmforth, Tom, "Russians of Narva Not Seeking 'Liberation' by Moscow," Radio Free Europe/Radio Liberty, April 4, 2014. As of June 20, 2016:
http://www.rferl.org/content/russia-estonia-not-crimea/25321328.html

Bartles, Charles, and Roger McDermott, "Russia's Military Operation in Crimea," *Problems of Post-Communism*, Vol. 61, No. 6, 2014, pp. 57–58.

BBC, "Estonia's Ruling Party Wins Election Victory," March 2, 2015a.

BBC, "Russia Jails Estonia Security Official Eston Kohver," August 19, 2015b. As of June 20, 2016:
http://www.bbc.com/news/world-europe-33986733

Bershidsky, Leonid, "Estonia Can Handle Putin's Soft Power," *BloombergView*, March 2, 2015. As of June 20, 2016:
http://www.bloombergview.com/articles/2015-03-02/estonia-can-handle-putin-s-soft-power

Bertelsmann Stiftung, "BTI 2014—Latvia Country Report," 2014.

Bērziņš, Jānis, "Russia's New Generation Warfare in Ukraine: Implications for Latvian Defense Policy," National Defence Academy of Latvia, Center for Security and Strategic Research, Policy Paper No. 2, April 2014.

Bodner, Matthew, "Kremlin Threatens Response to U.S. Nuclear Bomb Deployment in Germany," *The Moscow Times,* September 23, 2015. As of June 20, 2016:
http://www.themoscowtimes.com/business/article/kremlin-threatens-response-to-us-nuclear-bomb-deployment-in-germany/535106.html

Brüggemann, Karsten, and Andres Kasekamp, "The Politics of History and the 'War of Monuments' in Estonia," *Nationalities Papers*, Vol. 36, No. 3, July 2008, pp. 427–448.

Bugriy, Maksym, "Konstantin Malofeev: Fringe Christian Orthodox Financier of the Donbas Separatists," The Jamestown Foundation. August 8, 2014. As of June 20, 2016: http://www.jamestown.org/programs/edm/single/?tx_ttnews%5Btt_news%5D=42725&cHash=58def74e6315f226d043d9270402ebb5#.Vi8S9H6rTRY

Central Statistics Bureau of Latvia, 2014 and 2015 data. As of June 20, 2016: http://www.csb.gov.lv/en/dati/statistics-database-30501.html

Charap, Samuel, "Ghosts of Hybrid War," *Survival*, Vol. 57, No. 6, December 2015–January 2016.

Chekinov, Sergei, and Sergei Bogdonov, "The Nature and Content of a New-Generation War," *Military Thought*, No. 4, 2013, pp. 12–23.

Chivvis, Christopher S., Raphael S. Cohen, Bryan Frederick, Daniel S. Hamilton, F. Stephen Larrabee, and Bonny Lin, *NATO's Northeastern Flank: Emerging Opportunities for Engagement*, Santa Monica, Calif.: RAND Corporation, RR-1467-AF, forthcoming.

Cianetti, Licia, "The Governing Parties Survived Latvia's Election, but the Issue of the Country's Russian-Speaking Minority Remains Centre-Stage," London School of Economics and Political Science, October 8, 2014. As of June 20, 2016: http://blogs.lse.ac.uk/europpblog/2014/10/08/the-governing-parties-survived-latvias-election-but-the-issue-of-the-countrys-russian-speaking-minority-remains-centre-stage/

Coalson, Robert, "Top Russian General Lays Bare Putin's Plan for Ukraine," *The World Post*, September 2, 2014. As of June 20, 2016: http://www.huffingtonpost.com/robert-coalson/valery-gerasimov-putin-ukraine_b_5748480.html

Cohen, Ariel, "Putin Explores Legal Loopholes to Take Back the Baltic Nations," *Newsweek*, July 16, 2015. As of June 20, 2016: http://www.newsweek.com/putin-explores-legal-loopholes-take-back-baltic-nations-354379

Collier, Mike, with Mary Sibierski, "NATO Allies Come to Grips with Russia's 'Hybrid Warfare,'" AFP, March 18, 2015. As of June 20, 2016: http://news.yahoo.com/nato-allies-come-grips-russias-hybrid-warfare-182821895.html

Covington, S. R., *Putin's Choice for Russia*, Cambrige, Mass.: Harvard Kennedy School, Belfer Center for Science and International Affairs, August 2015.

Duina, Francesco, and Carlo Miani, "Fitting in the Baltics: National Identity, Minorities and Compliance with EU Accession Requirements in Lithuania and Latvia," *Comparative European Politics,* Vol. 13, No. 5, September 2015, pp. 535–552.

Ehala, Martin, "The Bronze Soldier: Identity Threat and Maintenance in Estonia," *Journal of Baltic Studies*, Vol. 40, No. 1, 2009, pp. 142–143, 152–155.

Estonia Internal Security Service, *Annual Report 2013*.

Estonia.eu, "Russian-Language Schools' Transition to Partial Estonian-Language Instruction—What Is Happening and Why?" January 31, 2013. As of June 20, 2016: http://estonia.eu/about-estonia/society/russian-language-schools-transition-to-partial-estonian-language-instruction-what-is-happening-and-why.html

Estonia.eu, "Citizenship," August 10, 2015. As of June 20, 2016: http://estonia.eu/about-estonia/society/citizenship.html

European Union Agency for Fundamental Rights, *European Union Minorities and Discrimination Survey: Main Results Report*, 2009. As of June 20, 2016: http://fra.europa.eu/en/publication/2012/eu-midis-main-results-report

Faiola, Anthony, "Ukraine Mobilizes Reservists but Relies on Diplomacy," *Washington Post*, March 17, 2014.

Farmer, Ben, and David Blair, "Estonia Stages Biggest Military Exercise in Country's History Amid Fears of Russian 'Aggression,'" *The Telegraph*, May 12, 2015. As of June 20, 2016: http://www.telegraph.co.uk/news/worldnews/europe/estonia/11600458/Estonia-stages-biggest-military-exercise-in-countrys-history-amid-fears-of-Russian-aggression.html

Finley, J. C., "Ukrainian President Announces Creation of National Guard, Mobilization of Armed Forces," UPI, March 11, 2014. As of June 20, 2016: http://www.upi.com/Top_News/World-News/2014/03/11/Ukrainian-president-announces-creation-of-national-guard-mobilization-of-armed-forces/4641394545650/

Flintoff, Corey, "Estonia 'Spy' Dispute Could Be Russia Making Anti-NATO Mischief," *NPR*, September 14, 2014. As of June 20, 2016: http://www.npr.org/2014/09/14/348351241/estonia-spy-dispute-could-be-russia-making-anti-nato-mischief

Foster, Brian R., *Enhancing the Efficiency of NATO Intelligence Under an ASG-I*, Carlisle Barracks, Pa.: U.S. Army War College, Strategy Research Project, 2013.

Galeotti, Mark, "The 'Gerasimov Doctrine' and Russian Non-Linear War," *In Moscow's Shadow* (blog), July 6, 2014. As of June 20, 2016: https://inmoscowsshadows.wordpress.com/2014/07/06/the-gerasimov-doctrine-and-russian-non-linear-war/

Galeotti, Mark, "Organized Crime in the Baltics States," *Baltic Review*, March 24, 2015. As of June 20, 2016: http://baltic-review.com/organized-crime-in-the-baltic-states/

Gorenburg, Dmitry, "Moscow Conference on International Security 2015, Part 2: Gerasimov on Military Threats Facing Russia," *Russian Military Reform*, May 4, 2015. As of June 20, 2016:
https://russiamil.wordpress.com/2015/05/04/moscow-conference-on-international-security-2015-part-2-gerasimov-on-military-threats-facing-russia/

Grigas, Agnia, "The New Generation of Baltic Russian Speakers," EurActiv.com, November 28, 2014. As of June 20, 2016:
http://www.euractiv.com/sections/europes-east/new-generation-baltic-russian-speakers-310405

Grigas, Agnia, *Beyond Crimea: The New Russian Empire*, New Haven, Conn.: Yale University Press, 2016.

Hansen, Holley, "Ethnic Voting and Representation: Minority Russians in Post-Soviet States," Ph.D. dissertation, University of Iowa, 2009.

Herszenhorn, David, "Latvians Reject Russian as Second Language," *New York Times*, February 19, 2012.

Herszenhorn, David, and Peter Baker, "Russia Steps Up Help for Rebels in Ukraine War," *New York Times*, July 25, 2014.

Higgins, Andrew, "Latvian Region Has Distinct Identity, and Allure for Russia," *New York Times*, May 20, 2015.

Hille, Kathrin, "Russia Censors Discussion of Involvement in Ukraine," *Financial Times*, May 28, 2015.

Hoffman, Frank, "Hybrid Warfare and Challenges," *Joint Forces Quarterly*, Vol. 52, No. 1, 2009, p. 34.

Hoffman, Frank, "On Not-So-New Warfare: Political Warfare vs. Hybrid Threats," *War on the Rocks*, July 28, 2014.

Hurt, Martin, *Lessons Identified in Crimea: Does Estonia's National Defence Model Meet Our Needs?* Tallinn, Estonia: International Centre for Defence and Security, April 2014. As of June 20, 2016:
http://www.icds.ee/fileadmin/media/icds.ee/failid/Martin%20Hurt%20-%20Lessons%20Identified%20in%20Crimea.pdf

Hyndle-Hussein, Joanna, "The New Government in Estonia," Center for Eastern Studies (OSW), November 30, 2016. As of January 4, 2017:
https://www.osw.waw.pl/en/publikacje/analyses/2016-11-30/new-government-estonia

Internal Revenue Service, "Yearly Average Currency Exchange Rates," 2016. As of June 20, 2016:
https://www.irs.gov/Individuals/International-Taxpayers/Yearly-Average-Currency-Exchange-Rates

International Crisis Group, "The Ukraine Crisis: Risks of Renewed Military Conflict After Minsk II," Crisis Group Europe Briefing No. 73, April 1, 2015.

International Institute for Strategic Studies, *The Military Balance*, 2015.

Ioffe, Julia, "Ethnic Russians in the Baltics Are Actually Persecuted. So Why Isn't Putin Stepping In?" *New Republic*, March 11, 2014. As of June 20, 2016:
http://www.newrepublic.com/article/116970/estonia-lithuania-mistreat-ethnic-russians-nato-keeps-putin-out

Jane's World Armies, "Estonia," 2015.

Jane's World Armies, "Latvia," 2015.

Jones, Sam, "Ukraine: Russia's New Art of War," *Financial Times*, August 28, 2014. As of June 20, 2016:
http://www.ft.com/intl/cms/s/2/ea5e82fa-2e0c-11e4-b760-00144feabdc0.html

Jones, Sam, "Estonia Ready to Deal with Little Green Men," *Financial Times*, May 13, 2015.

Jozwiak, Rikard, "EU Plans to Step Up Fight Against Russian Propaganda," Radio Free Europe/Radio Liberty, June 24, 2015. As of June 20, 2016:
http://www.rferl.org/content/european-union-russia-propoganda-georgia-moldova-/27091155.html

Kaminski, Matthew, "The Town Where the Russian Dilemma Lives," *Wall Street Journal,* July 4, 2014. As of June 20, 2016:
http://online.wsj.com/articles/matthew-kaminski-the-town-where-the-russian-dilemma-lives-1404510023

Kasekamp, Andres, *A History of the Baltics*, New York: Palgrave Macmillan, 2010.

Keck, Zachery, "Russia Threatens to Deploy Nuclear Weapons in Crimea," *National Interest*, June 1, 2015. As of June 20, 2016:
http://nationalinterest.org/blog/the-buzz/russia-threatens-deploy-nuclear-weapons-crimea-13013

Kivirähk, Juhan, "Integrating Estonia's Russian-Speaking Population: Findings of National Defense Opinion Surveys," Tallinn, Estonia: International Centre for Defence and Security, December 2014, pp. 8–9.

Kivirähk, Juhan, "Public Opinion and National Defence," Estonian Ministry of Defence, April 2015. As of June 20, 2016:
http://www.kaitseministeerium.ee/sites/default/files/elfinder/article_files/public_opinion_and_national_defence_2015_march_0.pdf

Knoema, "Leningrad Region—Gross Regional Product Per Capita," multiple years. As of June 20, 2016:
http://knoema.com/atlas/Russian-Federation/Leningrad-Region/GRP-per-capita

Knoema, "Pskov Region—Gross Regional Product Per Capita," multiple years. As of June 20, 2016:
http://knoema.com/atlas/Russian-Federation/Pskov-Region/topics/Gross-regional-product/Gross-regional-product/GRP-per-capita

Kofman, Michael, "Russian Hybrid Warfare and Other Dark Arts," *War on the Rocks,* March 11, 2016. As of June 20, 2016:
http://warontherocks.com/2016/03/russian-hybrid-warfare-and-other-dark-arts/

Kofman, Michael, and Matthew Rojansky, "A Closer Look at Russia's 'Hybrid War,'" Woodrow Wilson Center Kennan Cable No. 7, April 2015.

Kravchenko, Stepan, "The Rebel Leader Who Makes Putin Look Cautious," *Bloomberg*, February 4, 2015. As of June 20, 2016:
http://www.bloomberg.com/news/articles/2015-02-04/russian-fire-starter-says-putin-now-hostage-to-ukraine-war

Kudelia, Serhiy, "Domestic Sources of the Donbas Insurgency," PONARS Eurasia Policy Memo, September 2014.

Lagerspetz, Mikko, "Cultural Autonomy of National Minorities in Estonia: The Erosion of a Promise," *Journal of Baltic Studies*, Vol. 45, No. 4, 2014, pp. 457–475.

Laitin, David, *Identity in Formation*, Ithaca, N.Y.: Cornell University Press, 1998.

"Latvia's Election: How to Deal with Harmony," *The Economist*, October 5, 2014. As of June 20, 2016:
http://www.economist.com/blogs/easternapproaches/2014/10/latvias-election?zid=307&ah=5e80419d1bc9821ebe173f4f0f060a07

Latvia Security Police, *Annual Report 2013*.

Latvijas Republikas Saeima, "Saeima Adopts Provisions on Recognition of Dual Citizenship," May 9, 2013. As of June 20, 2016:
http://www.saeima.lv/en/news/saeima-news/20957-saeima-adopts-provisions-on-recognition-of-dual-citizenship

Lawless Latvia, website, no date. As of June 20, 2016:
http://www.lawlesslatvia.com/

Luhn, Alec "Fight Club, Donetsk," *Foreign Policy,* June 16, 2014.

Luxmoore, Matthew, "Latvia Struggles with Restive Russian Minority Amid Regional Tensions," *Al Jazeera America*, June 13, 2015. As of June 20, 2016:
http://america.aljazeera.com/articles/2015/6/13/latvia-resists-russian-soft-power.html

Maigre, Merle, "Nothing New in Hybrid Warfare: The Estonian Experience and Recommendations for NATO," German Marshall Fund of the United States, February 2015.

Martyn-Hemphill, Richard, "Estonia's New Premier Comes From Party with Links to Russia," *New York Times*, November 20, 2016. As of January 4, 2017:
http://www.nytimes.com/2016/11/21/world/europe/estonia-juri-ratas-center-party.html

Mastriano, Douglas, "Defeating Putin's Strategy of Ambiguity," *War on the Rocks*, November 6, 2014. As of June 20, 2016:
http://warontherocks.com/2014/11/defeating-putins-strategy-of-ambiguity/

Milne, Richard, "Party with Ties to Putin Pushes Ahead in Estonian Polls," *Financial Times*, February 27, 2015.

NATO, "The North Atlantic Treaty," April 4, 1949. As of June 20, 2016:
http://www.nato.int/cps/en/natohq/official_texts_17120.htm

NATO, "New Satellite Imagery Exposes Russian Combat Troops Inside Ukraine," August 28, 2014a. As of June 20, 2016:
http://aco.nato.int/new-satellite-imagery-exposes-russian-combat-troops-inside-ukraine.aspx

NATO, "Wales Summit Declaration," September 5, 2014b. As of June 20, 2016:
http://www.nato.int/cps/en/natohq/official_texts_112964.htm

NATO, "Defence Expenditures of NATO Countries (2008–2015)," January 28, 2016. As of June 20, 2016:
http://www.nato.int/nato_static_fl2014/assets/pdf/pdf_2016_01/20160129_160128-pr-2016-11-eng.pdf#page=2

"NATO Destabilizing Baltic by Stationing Nuke-Capable Aircraft—Moscow," *Russia Today*, December 1, 2014. As of June 20, 2016:
http://www.rt.com/news/210383-nato-baltic-troops-russia/

NATO Parliamentary Assembly Defence and Security Committee, "Hybrid Warfare: NATO's New Strategic Challenge?" Draft Report, April 7, 2015.

Nurick, Robert, and Magnus Nordenman, eds., "Nordic-Baltic Security in the 21st Century: The Regional Agenda and the Global Role," *The Atlantic Council*, September 2011.

Oliker, Olga, "Russia's New Military Doctrine: Same as the Old Doctrine, Mostly," *Washington Post*, January 15, 2015.

Oliker, Olga, Keith Crane, Lowell H. Schwartz, and Catherine Yusupov, *Russian Foreign Policy: Sources and Implications*, Santa Monica, Calif.: RAND Corporation, MG-768-AF, 2009. As of June 20, 2016:
http://www.rand.org/pubs/monographs/MG768.html

O'Loughlin, John, and Gerard Toal, "Mistrust About Political Motives in Contested Ukraine," *Washington Post*, February 13, 2015.

"On the Border," *The Economist*, March 5, 2015. As of June 20, 2016:
http://www.economist.com/news/europe/21645845-how-nervousness-over-russia-affects-daily-life-and-politics-border

Osburg, Jan, *Unconventional Options for the Defense of the Baltic States: The Swiss Approach*, Santa Monica, Calif.: RAND Corporation, PE-179-RC, 2016. As of June 20, 2016:
http://www.rand.org/pubs/perspectives/PE179.html

Person, Robert, "6 Reasons Not to Worry About Russia Invading the Baltics," *Washington Post*, November 12, 2015.

Pifer, Steven, and Hannah Thoburn, "Nuanced Views in Eastern Ukraine," *Brookings*, April 28, 2014. As of June 20, 2016:
http://www.brookings.edu/blogs/up-front/posts/2014/04/28-nuanced-views-eastern-ukraine-pifer-thoburn

Pindják, Peter, "Deterring Hybrid Warfare: A Chance for NATO and the EU to Work Together?" *NATO Review*, 2014. As of June 20, 2016:
http://www.nato.int/docu/review/2014/also-in-2014/Deterring-hybrid-warfare/EN/index.htm

Pukhov, Ruslan, "Nothing 'Hybrid' About Russia's War in Ukraine," *The Moscow Times*, May 27, 2015. As of June 20, 2016:
http://www.themoscowtimes.com/opinion/article/nothing-hybrid-about-russia-s-war-in-ukraine/522471.html

"Ratas: Estonian Center Party's Agreement with United Russia Is Non-Active," *Posttimees,* November 10, 2016. As of January 4, 2017:
http://news.postimees.ee/3905231/ratas-estonian-center-party-s-agreement-with-united-russia-is-non-active

"Riigikogu Simplifies Granting Estonian Citizenship to Children and Elderly," *The Baltic Course*, January 22, 2015. As of June 20, 2016:
http://www.baltic-course.com/eng/legislation/?doc=101394

Roth, Andrew, "From Russia, 'Tourists' Stir the Protests," *New York Times*, March 3, 2014.

Roth, Andrew, "Former Russian Rebels Trade War in Ukraine for Posh Life in Moscow," *Washington Post,* September 16, 2015.

Russian Federation, "On the Russian Federation's National Security Strategy," December 31, 2015, copy with author.

Schadlow, Nadia, "The Problem with Hybrid Warfare," *War on the Rocks*, April 2, 2015. As of June 20, 2016:
http://warontherocks.com/2015/04/the-problem-with-hybrid-warfare/

Schmitt, Eric, and Steve Lee Myers, "NATO Refocuses on the Kremlin, Its Original Foe," *New York Times*, June 23, 2015.

Shlapak, David A., and Michael Johnson, *Reinforcing Deterrence on NATO's Eastern Flank: Wargaming the Defense of the Baltics*, Santa Monica, Calif.: RAND Corporation, Santa Monica, Calif., RR-1253-A, 2015. As of June 20, 2016:
http://www.rand.org/pubs/research_reports/RR1253.html

Smith-Spark, Laura, Alla Eshchenko, and Emma Burrows, "Russia Was Ready to Put Nuclear Forces on Alert over Crimea, Putin Says," *CNN*, March 16, 2015. As of June 20, 2016:
http://www.cnn.com/2015/03/16/europe/russia-putin-crimea-nuclear/

Statistical Office of Estonia, Statistics Database, 2015. As of June 20, 2016:
http://www.stat.ee/database

Statistical Office of Estonia, Central Statistical Bureau of Latvia, and Statistics Lithuania, "2011 Population and Housing Censuses in Estonia, Latvia, and Lithuania," 2015. As of June 20, 2016:
http://www.stat.ee/dokumendid/220923

Stuttaford, Andrew, "On Shooting 'Little Green Men,'" *National Review*, May 14, 2015. As of June 20, 2016:
http://www.nationalreview.com/corner/418350/shooting-little-green-men-andrew-stuttaford

Sutyagin, Igor, "Russian Forces in Ukraine," RUSI Briefing paper, March 2015.

Svan, Jennifer. "US A-10s Arrive in Estonia for 6 Month Rotation," *Stars and Stripes,* September 22, 2015. As of June 20, 2016:
http://www.stripes.com/news/us-a-10s-arrive-in-estonia-for-6-month-rotation-1.369459

Tatham, Steve, "The Solution to Russian Propaganda Is Not EU or NATO Propaganda but Advanced Social Science to Understand and Mitigate Its Effect in Targeted Populations," *National Defense Academy of Latvia*, Policy Paper No. 4, July 2015.

Tikk, Eneken, Kadri Kaska, and Liis Vihul, "International Cyber Incidents: Legal Considerations," Tallinn, Estonia: Cooperative Cyber Defence Centre of Excellence (CCD COE), 2010. As of June 20, 2016:
https://ccdcoe.org/publications/books/legalconsiderations.pdf

Trei, Lisa, "Estonian Towns Vote for Autonomy," *The Moscow Times*, July 20, 1993. As of June 20, 2016:
http://www.themoscowtimes.com/sitemap/free/1993/7/article/estonian-towns-vote-for-autonomy/217775.html

Troianovski, Anton, "Germany Seeks to Counter Russian 'Propaganda' in Baltics," *Wall Street Journal*, April 17, 2015. As of June 20, 2016:
http://www.wsj.com/articles/germany-seeks-to-counter-russian-propaganda-in-baltics-1429294362

"TV in Russian: Estonia Leads the Way," *The Baltic Review*, August 20, 2015.

"'Unprecedented and Dangerous Step': Russia Slams NATO Troop Build-Up," *Russia Today*, April 2, 2015. As of June 20, 2016:
http://www.rt.com/news/246321-russia-nato-troops-border/

U.S. Army Special Operations Command, "Counter-Unconventional Warfare White Paper," September 26, 2014.

"US Commander Says NATO Will Bolster Intelligence-Sharing Among Military Alliance's Members," Associated Press, April 30, 2015.

Van Puyvelde, Damien, "Hybrid War, Does It Even Exist," *NATO Review*, 2015. As of June 20, 2016:
http://www.nato.int/docu/review/2015/Also-in-2015/hybrid-modern-future-warfare-russia-ukraine/EN/index.htm

Weaver, Courtney, "Malofeev: The Russian Billionaire Linking Moscow to the Rebels," *Financial Times,* July 24, 2014.

Weaver, Courtney, "Nemtsov's Final Report Says 220 Russian Troops Have Died in Ukraine," *Financial Times*, May 12, 2015.

"What's My Language?" *The Economist*, February 14, 2012. As of June 20, 2016:
http://www.economist.com/blogs/easternapproaches/2012/02/latvias-referendum

Wilson, Andrew, *Virtual Politics: Faking Democracy in the Post-Soviet World*, New Haven, Conn.: Yale University Press, 2005.

Winnerstig, Mike, ed., *Tools of Destabilization: Russian Soft Power and Non-Military Influence in the Baltic States*, Sweden Defense Research Agency (FOI), December 2014. As of June 20, 2016:
http://www.foi.se/rapport?rNo=FOI-R--3990--SE

World Bank, "GINI Index (World Bank Estimate)," 2016. As of June 20, 2016:
http://data.worldbank.org/indicator/SI.POV.GINI

Xil, "Russians in Baltic States (2011)," no date. As of June 20, 2016:
https://commons.wikimedia.org/wiki/File:Russians_in_Baltic_States_(2011).svg#/media/File:Russians_in_Baltic_States_(2011).svg

Zhukov, Yuri M., "Rust Belt Rebellion: The Economics Behind Eastern Ukraine's Upheaval," *Foreign Affairs*, Vol. 93, No. 3, June 2014.